I0643882

Keka‘a: The Making and Saving of North Beach West Maui

Keka'a: The Making and Saving of North Beach West Maui

Sydney Lehua Iaukea

Foreword by Lance D. Collins

North Beach-West Maui
Benefit Fund Inc.

Lahaina, Maui, Hawai'i

Printed in the United States of America

Includes bibliographical references and index.
ISBN 978-0-8248-5143-9

This book is printed on acid-free paper
and meets the guidelines for permanence and
durability of the Council on Library Resources.

Cover photo: Kaanapali Landing; Kaanapali, Maui, Hawaii. ca. 1930. Unknown photographer, Inter-Island Airways. Courtesy of Bishop Museum

This book was designed and composited by JM.cO Designs - jmcodesigns@gmail.com for the North Beach-West Maui Benefit Fund.

Distributed by University of Hawai'i Press
2840 Kolowalu Street
Honolulu, Hawai'i 96822-1888
www.uhpress.hawaii.edu

For my long line of moʻokūʻauhau on Maui,
and your presence—watching, protecting, and standing tall—in the landscapes and seascapes of this special island, Mahalo Nui.

Thank you to Craig Howes, Lance Collins, the West Maui Preservation Association, and the numerous activists and community members who stood and spoke for Kekaʻa.
Finally, to my mom and sister—Imua.

Contents

Foreword

The North Beach West Maui Benefit Fund, Inc., was established as a result of the intervention of the West Maui Preservation Association in the Special Management Area use permit application for the development of Lot 2 of the North Beach subdivision, as part of the settlement agreement between the West Maui Preservation Association and the developers of North Beach.

The West Maui Preservation Association had been organized to preserve, protect and restore the natural and cultural environment of West Maui including land conservation and educational activities. It intervened in the Special Management Area use permit applications for the development of Lot 2, Lot 3 and Lot 4 of the North Beach subdivision. It successfully established programs for proper drainage, water quality monitoring, dunes preservation and management, protecting ocean resources, banning pile driving, and mitigating traffic congestion.

In 1972, the U.S. Congress adopted the Coastal Zone

Management Act which instituted national policies regarding the preservation, protection and restoration of the natural resources within the coastal zone, and required states to establish Coastal Zone Management Plans. The Hawai'i State Legislature implemented a state coastal zone management regime with the objective that state action within the coastal zone give "full consideration to ecological, cultural, historic, esthetic, recreational, scenic, and open space values, and coastal hazards, as well as to needs for economic development." Haw. Rev. Stat. 205A-4

In addition to the Coastal Zone Management framework, the Hawai'i State Legislature established "special management areas" within the shoreline of the Coastal Zone "to avoid permanent losses of valuable resources and the foreclosure of management options, and to ensure that adequate access, by dedication or other means, to public owned or used beaches, recreation areas, and natural reserves is provided." Hawaii Revised Statutes §205A-21. In Maui County, the Planning Commissions are the designated authorities for the special management areas.

The North Beach West Maui Benefit Fund has committed to preserving and perpetuating the histories of West Maui in all its conflicting forms. At its inaugural meeting, the Fund committed to including the history of the development of North Beach itself. In many ways, the history of North Beach is the story of change in West Maui and the story of West Maui. Yet, as Dr. Iaukea demonstrates, the story of North Beach is also unique.

This volume is the latest in a series of projects to help expand the base of knowledge and understanding of West Maui's history, to help support planning for the possibilities of the present and the future.

Lance D. Collins, PhD
Ka'anapali, Maui

Introduction

At the age of just nineteen, right out of high school and a year of study at Maui Community College, I decided to go to work at the hotels in West Maui. I first worked as a spa attendant at the Hyatt, Ka'anapali. This didn't last long as the unofficial job description was to hold umbrellas over tourists, when it was raining, as they navigated the open-air lobby en-route to their hotel rooms. I didn't want to make small talk and have to apologize for the rain that fell unwelcomed on their vacations. I left soon after.

I then went to work as a hostess and cocktail waitress at the Sheraton, Maui. The money was good and I enjoyed working with the bartenders and my fellow co-workers. That was, until an old-timer yelled at me one New Year's Eve and I ended up in tears. This experience, coupled with the "How to be Aloha" classes we were compelled to attend, sent me back to school with a vengeance and much relief to have escaped. I was deeply disturbed by these experiences, but not able to adequately formalize or articulate the problem. It would be many years before I could put into words the discomfort I felt for being treated like a servant, and told to do so with a smile on my face and aloha in my heart. I have been critical of the tourism industry ever since.

Acknowledging this, my prerogative is one of no-growth, no development in general, especially when it comes to hotels and condominiums on sacred ʻāina and overpopulated places. This is not what occurred at North Beach, an area just north of Kaʻanapali. The Hawaiian name for this ʻāina is Kekaʻa, and it was an important site for kānaka maoli over many generations. Culturally and politically significant, Kekaʻa was at one time the capital of the Hawaiian Islands.

Pioneer Mill gained controlled of vast amounts of land in West Maui a century and a half ago to facilitate their sugar plantation. Much of this land, and the ready-made labor force initiated on the fields, were then transitioned to accommodate the all-encompassing tourism industry on Maui. In the process, Kekaʻa underwent a myriad of changes, not unlike other places in Hawaiʻi. Narrated here are the ways this ʻåina has been utilized—from kānaka maoli land use, to sugar plantation and a brief intermission as an airport, to the most recent landscape and backdrop for hotels and condominiums for Maui's continually growing tourism industry.

In general, development on Maui has not waned from a dependency model, one that would give concessions to big business and rely on submissive community support. However, the negative results of this history were being realized in the early 1990s, and so community involvement ramped up—with Kekaʻa serving as a site for the convergence. The negotiations for this area changed the discourse on Maui so that not just how we were developing, but why and for whom, became relevant questions. Many found that by insisting on cultural and environmental imperatives, the development rhetoric and unrestrained growth model was questioned and contained.

This book looks at how this area was ultimately accomodated for tourism. And because of community activism, what occurred here was a downgraded version of the original projection—to become another Ka‘anapali, Hawai‘i’s first master planned resort. The multiple negotiations, interventions, and settlements by the first intervenors, and by the West Maui Preservation Association (WMPA), ultimately helped to contain this massive development path, and instead paved the way for community input in the overall development process on Maui. How these community voices are valued in future developments remains to be seen.

Chapter 1: The Lahaina District

The Lahaina District stretches across the entire landmass of West Maui and contains the wahi pana (sacred sites), makani (winds), wai and kai (fresh and sea water), and the moʻolelo (stories and narratives) of generations of kānaka maoli (Hawaiians) from Maui. The literal meaning of Lahaina is "cruel sun" because of the hot weather and droughts that plague the area. Hua, the chief of Lahaina, killed his kahuna and caused the droughts:

> Hua figures prominently in Hawaii and Maui traditions, the one here referred to being: in a dispute with his priest and prophet Luahoomoe, on East Maui, about some uwau birds, he became so angry that he vowed death to the priest. Aware of his coming fate Luahoomoe directed his sons to safety while he perished in flames. Immediately the rains ceased, streams and springs dried up so that famine and desolation spread, from the continuous drought. Hua died miserably from which comes the saying: 'Rattling are the bones of Hua in the sun.'[1]

Another name for Lahaina is Honoapiʻilani (bays of Chief Piʻilani). Piʻilani ruled Molokaʻi, Lānaʻi, and Kahoʻolawe, and

---

1 Compiled by Elspeth P. Sterling, *Sites of Maui*, A. Fornander, Collection 5:660. (Honolulu, Hawaiʻi: Bishop Museum Press, 1998), 18.

these islands could all be seen from Lahaina.[2] The bays of Pi'ilani are located north of Lahaina, just past Ka'anapali, and they are Honokōwai, Honokeana, Honokahua, Honolua, Honokōhau, and Hononana.[3] Lele was another original name for Lahaina, noted for the piece of the kuleana land that sits near the shore.[4] These multiple names are documented in Sterling's *Sites of Maui*: "Lahaina is said by early native writers to have had two other names in ancient times, it being first known as Honoapi'ilani. Subsequently this was changed to Lele, and in later times to Lahaina—as known to this day."[5] But perhaps the earliest name for Lahaina is Ihikapalaumaewa, after a child of Papa and Wākea.[6]

Today, the entire west side of Maui is recognized as the Lahaina district. The enormity of this district came about through multiple changes in Hawaiian land tenure proceedings. Beginning in 1859, the Civil Code narrowed the twelve districts of Maui to four. For West Maui, the Lahaina district combined the Ka'anapali district with the Lahaina district and the island

---

2 Van James, *Ancient Sites of Maui, Moloka'i, and Lāna'i: Archaeological Places of Interest in the Hawaiian Islands* (Honolulu: Mutual Publishing, 2001), 37.

3 Jocelyn Fujii, *Kapalua Nui: Place of Life* (Honolulu: Hula Moon Press, 2008).

4 Lele translates as "A detached part or lot of land belonging to one *'ili*, but located in another *'ili*." Mary Kawena Pukui and Samuel H. Elbert, *Hawaiian Dictionary* (Honolulu: University of Hawai'i Press, (1957) 1986), s.v. "lele."

5 Sterling (*Hawaiian Annual for 1908*, 21), 34.

6 Sterling (S.M. Kamakau, "Ka Moolelo o Hawaii," *Ke Au Okoa*, March 10, 1870. Trans. E.P. Sterling), 2.

of Kaho‘olawe.[7] The Lahaina District was further divided in 1896 and subdivisions were implemented. These were the subdivisions:

Subdivision of Lahaina District

No. 1
Kahakuloa including Makaluia, Honokohau, and Honolua to the fence separating Honolua from Honokahua.
Enumerator, D. Taylor Jr.

No. 2
All that part of Kaanapali extending from the fence separating Honolua from Honokahua to Kekaa (Black Rock) including the Plantation settlement on the Kula back of Kekaa.
Enumerator, E. Reimann

No. 3
All that part of Lahaina on the Kaanapali side of the Old Lahainaluna Road including Kahoma valley, Lahainaluna valley, and Keawawa.
Enumerator, C.B. Cockett

No. 4
All that part of Lahaina on the Olowalu side of the Old Lahainaluna Road including Kauaula Valley.
Enumerator, D.H. Kahaulelio

7 Sterling (R.D. King, Districts in the Hawaiian Islands, in J.W. Coulter, *A Gazatteer of the Territory of Hawaii*, 1935, 216-217), 3.

No. 5
Olowalu and Ukumehame
Enumerator, Noah Kahaulelio

No. 6
The Island of Lanai
Enumerator, Solomon Kahoohalahe[8]

After these subdivisions were recognized, the Session Laws of 1909 designated the islands of Maui, Moloka'i, Lāna'i, and Kaho'olawe into six districts. In regards to Lahaina, it was declared that "all that portion of Maui west of Wailuku district including the island of Lanai, to be styled the Lahaina district."[9] "West of Wailuku" makes up the entire po'o (head) of the island of Maui.[10] Kaho'olawe was redesignated to the Makawao district in this land division. In its entirety, the Lahaina district lies vast and open against the West Maui Mountains. The following photographs illuminate the breadth and beauty of this area.

---

8 "General Correspondence, Incoming Letters of the Board of Education 1896, Maui, June-August," 261-33-2, Hawai'i State Archives, Honolulu, Hawai'i.

9 Sterling (R.D. King, Districts in the Hawaiian Islands, in J.W. Coulter, *Gazatteer*, 216-217), 4.

10 The Island of Maui resembles a woman breastfeeding her baby. The top of the po'o, or head, of the woman comprises a large portion of the Lahaina district.

Aerial view of West Maui with the island of Lanai in the background; Maui, Hawaii. January 27, 1953. Courtesy of Bishop Museum

"Pioneer Mill. Lahaina" Pioneer Mill; Lahaina, Maui, Hawaii. ca. 1915. Courtesy of Bishop Museum

Aerial view of West Maui mountains, Hawaii. Photo by Ray Jerome Baker. Courtesy of Bishop Museum

The west end of Maui from the air; Maui, Hawaii. Photo by Ray Jerome Baker. Courtesy of Bishop Museum

West Maui coastline from Maalaea to Olowalu; Maui, Hawaii. ca. 1930. Courtesy of Bishop Museum

Dedication of the tunnel in the highway to Lahaina; Olowalu, Maui, Hawaii. This was the first tunnel in a public road, for civilian vehicles, in Hawaii. 1951. Courtesy of Bishop Museum

"Lonely palm looking toward the mountains". Courtesy of Bishop Museum

In 1881, Sereno E. Bishop was tasked with surveying the Lahaina district for the Hawaiian Government Survey. During this time, surveying the landscape occurred across the Hawaiian Kingdom terrain so that boundaries and Mahele land awards could be clarified. Besides land deeds and boundaries, the earlier 1846 survey of Lahaina documented both a large population and a robust economy. This was attributed to the influence of the whaling industry in Lahaina before its fall. By the time the Sereno survey was released in 1884, the population and economy had changed drastically in Lahaina:

> By 1884, however, its population had fallen to approximately one thousand as indicated by the reduced number of dwellings Bishop mapped. The many vacant properties would suggest that they were abandoned or leased. Lahaina's former importance is reflected in the presence of a few cultural artifacts of significance, namely a courthouse and a prison one block mauka of it. The school at Lahainaluna was the anchor of the long involvement of missionaries in Lahaina, and houses identified with the names of the several missionary families show that they were still there in 1884. Indeed, by this time the children of many of those families were beginning to dominate the plantation economy. The Pioneer Inn, a major tourist attraction in Lahaina today, is sited on what Bishop's map identifies as a taro patch.[11]

---

11 Riley Moore Moffat and Gary L. Fitzpatrick, *Mapping the Lands and Waters of Hawai'i: The Hawaiian Government Survey, Palapala'aina, Vol. 3* (Honolulu: Editions Limited, 2004), 52.

These surveys offered social commentary on the place. The maps themselves are testimony to the advanced and sophisticated land mapping projects in Hawai'i over a century and a half ago. Lahainaluna College, located above Lahaina town, was the site of this extensive and comprehensive study. Gary L. Fitzpatrick notes "The beginning of map compilation and printing at Lahainaluna has been hailed as the first creation of maps for the use and benefit of Hawaiians."[12] M. Puakea Nogelmeier writes "Education was in the Hawaiian language, and the reading of maps and the creation of new maps was soon an important part of the Hawaiian educational curriculum."[13] And,

> The introduction of western cartography could have easily eclipsed the traditional perspective, yet because Hawaiians were actively involved in the production of maps, traditional Hawaiian understanding, insight, and data were included in them. Hawaiian maps became a distillation of two worldviews, that included both outside and inside knowledge.[14]

In the 1830s, Lahainaluna was at the forefront of creating cartographic technology in Hawai'i. The students produced

12 Gary L. Fitzpatrick, "Mapmaking at Lahainaluna," In *He Mau Palapala Aina, A Me Na Niele e Pili Ana: Maps and Questions Regarding Them* (Honolulu: Hawaiian Historical Society, 2011), xix.

13 M. Puakea Nogelmeier, "Hawaiian Geography, Old and New," In *He Mau Palapala Aina, A Me Na Niele e Pili Ana: Maps and Questions Regarding Them* (Honolulu: Hawaiian Historical Society, 2011), xv.

14 Nogelmeier, xvi.

a co-articulation of ʻāina—the maps represented native understandings of place within a western medium. These maps were beneficial because they clearly delineated ka ʻāina according to Hawaiian understandings of place and within western scientific discourse.

Further, these maps were not just of ka pae ʻāina (Hawaiʻi), but were produced to represent all of the world's continents. Hawaiians saw themselves in relation to global populations and distant landmasses:

> In addition to compiling important maps of Hawaiʻi, the cartographers at Lahainaluna took on another difficult task: translating the place names of oceans, continents, countries, islands, states, cities, rivers, mountains, and other physical features of the earth into Hawaiian.[15]

How to distill and record what is essentially a fluid entity? That was their task—to record and represent the winds, rains, and seas that shape the place and inform the landscape.

The natural elements in Lahaina that had shaped the landscape for generations are known by multiple names and through different moʻolelo (narratives). The specific wind for Lahaina is the Kauaula wind: "The strong wind of Kawaula or Kauaula derives its name from the noted 'red' gorge, through which it rushes at times from the wooded peaks down upon

15 Fitzpatrick, xix.

Lahainaluna and Lahaina."[16] Besides this particular wind, *The Wind Gourd of La'amaomao* documents the many winds for the entire Lahaina district. The seas are also noted below from *Sites of Maui*. Both elements are described artistically:

> The kauaula wind has blown;
> It now murmurs among the cliffs
> Beyond the cliffs of Kahakuloa.
> The waiuli is next at Honolua.
> The pohakea is at Mahinahina,
> The lililehua is at Napali,
> The Kaimihau is of Kekaa,
> The nahua is at Kaanapali,
> The ululoa is of that section,
> The ma-a-a is of Lahaina,
> And floats above at Kamaiki,
> The cliff being awakened.
> The alani is of Liloa,
> The paalaa is of Makaha,
> The children of Ku, of Naiwi,
> The kaiaulu is at Pulupulu,
> Whirling madly along the plain,
> The holokaomi is of Paomai,
> It is the kupa, the okee wind,
> The pelu wind of the lowlands,
> The paiolua is on the ocean,
> Tis the moae and hoolua… [17]

---

16 Sterling (G.T. Lecker, Lahainaluna, 1831-1877, xiii), 30.

17 Sterling (J.J. Kanepuu, He Moolelo no Pakaa, *Ke Au Okoa*, Oct. 17, 1867), 7.

> Eight Seas:
> The expression eight seas admits of two meanings. It is said that when a Hawaiian at Lahaina speaks of the eights seas, he refers to the following channels:
> Between Lahaina and Molokai,
> Between Molokai and Lanai,
> Between Lanai and Kaluakoi,
> Between Lanai and Kahoolawe,
> Between Kahoolawe and Honuaula,
> Between Olualu and Kahoolawe,
> Between Lahaina and Lanai,
> Between Kahakuloa and Molokai
>
> But in other circumstances, when he refers to the eight seas of the whole groups of islands, they are as follows:
> Between Hawaii and Maui,
> Between Maui and Kahoolawe,
> Between Kahoolawe and Lanai,
> Between Lanai and Molokai,
> Between Molokai and Oahu,
> Between Oahu and Kauai,
> Between Kauai and Niihau,
> Between Niihau and Kaula[18]

The channels to Lāna'i and Moloka'i from Ka'anapali are the 'Au'au and Pailolo channels. And in days gone past, "Kiha-a-Pi'ilani, the son of Pi'ilani, is said to have surfed from this region of West Maui to Moloka'i across the Pailolo Channel."[19]

---

18 Sterling ("An Ode to the Soul," *The Polynesian,* July 11, 1840), 9.

19 Fujii, 16.

Today, these winds and seas continue to shape ka ʻāina, and knowing them is still relevant for the surfers, paddlers, voyagers, and fishermen from this area. This history of this ʻāina and people can be seen in petroglyphs, or kiʻi pōhaku, as these early markings depicted the tapestry of life. Found throughout Hawaiʻi, petroglyphs act as a primary storyteller by recording significant life and community events specific to each site. For this district, petroglyphs are found predominantly in the Olowalu and Maʻalaea areas. Walker makes note of such:

> Of an entirely different sort, two particularly interesting areas of these rock writings are to be found right in the middle of Pioneer Mill's cane fields near Lahaina. Of the two, the better known and more easily reached is in the Olowalu area, about a mile through the cane, mauka of the highway to Lahaina. Plainly seen, even from the access of the road, they're scratched in the bare stone sides of a hill. Further along, there's a heiau (temple) too.
>
> The Olowalu petroglyphs are of several types and of apparently different periods, some appearing fresher than others. The most recent were obviously made after the Hawaiians learned the written alphabet, as evidenced by names painstakingly carved above the older and more historical scratchings.[20]

---

20 Sterling (Jeanne Booth Johnson, "Maui's Past Shown in Stone," *The Honolulu Advertiser*, Hawaiian Holiday, Dec. 7, 1958, 14), 25.

More petroglyphs are found in Kahoma Valley:

> Less known and apparently of far older origin are petroglyphs of strictly matchstick type located on the side of a cliff up Kahoma Valley, just below Lahainaluna School. Also located on Pioneer Mill Co. property, they were recently rediscovered by J.B. McConkey, of Lahaina Light & Power Co. Ltd. Extending along the left side of the road, the figures are found at intervals for at least a sixth of a mile. Since the area has been relatively unexplored, it is believed that more of the figures exist behind the dense underbrush at the base of the cliff. Others probably exist on the buried faces of slate which have fallen from the parent cliff.[21]

The petroglyphs tell the stories of voyaging, taro cultivation, fishing, and farming. Lahaina town was also known as a city of refuge—where one could go to in order to escape persecution and judgment. Olowalu and Po'opu'upa'a at Waihe'e were other cities of refuge on Maui.[22]

From these mo'olelo, and from agricultual evidence, it is clear that the Lahaina district was agriculturally abundant and conducted immense fishing and taro cultivation. Ko'a, or fishing shrines, existed in Ma'alaea, and fishponds were prevalent in Lahaina and Mālā. Some of the heiau that accompanied these sites have survived, while most have not. Sugar cane fields now surround the remnants of the massive terraces that were used for taro cultivation. These massive terraces dried up because of

---

21 Sterling (Johnson, "Maui's Past Shown in Stone"), 42.

22 Sterling (*Ke Au Hou*, Sept. 21, 1910. MS SC Sterling 3.12.3.), 17.

the diversion of wai (fresh water) for the sugar cane fields. This fact is noted in Sterling's *Sites of Maui*, as relayed by Hanley's *Hawaiian Planter* book:

> The large streams named Kanaha and Kahoma, flowing out of the westward valleys of Kahoolewa Ridge, the eastward slopes of which drain into Iao Valley, formerly irrigated the most extensive plantations on this side of the island. All of this is now in sugar.[23]

Today, the Kahoma River is bone dry. And, most of the taro produced in this region is but a memory, with only traces of that economy still apparent:

> Above the Pioneer Plantation reservoirs, terraces cover the flatland just below the entrance to Ukumehame Canyon. Only a few of these are now under cultivation. The upper terraces have been long abandoned, and those just above the reservoirs are only half used—that half unsuccessfully, because of insufficient water for flooding. The terraces used to extend well down over the land below the valley, but, with the exception of one tiny taro plantation standing like an island in the midst of the cane, all vestiges of the ancient civilization have been plowed under. This is excellent wet taro soil.[24]

---

23 Sterling (E.S.C. Handy, *Hawaiian Planter*, 104-106), 36.

24 Sterling (E.S.C. Handy, *Hawaiian Planter*, 103), 20.

Wire fence along a sugarcane field; Hawaii. Photo by Ray Jerome Baker. Courtesy of Bishop Museum

Rock structure in a sugarcane field; Hawaii. Courtesy of Bishop Museum

Diverting water for sugar cultivation in Hawai'i has a lengthy social, political, and economic history. Controlling these waters still informs rights discourse, and symbolizes economic inequality in contemporary Hawai'i. The various fights to return the waters to their proper flows are ongoing on the island of Maui and elsewhere. The underlying imperative for farmers is that wai becomes accessible once again because wai is an important cultural and genealogical right. Returning the streams to their proper courses, and allowing access to farmers, is necessary for the health of the entire community. The history and politics of Pioneer Mill's diversion of wai in the Lahaina district, and the enormous impact of the sugar industry on Lahaina and Hawai'i as a whole, is further explored in the next chapter. But in regards to Lahaina town, as early as the 1860s sugar was regarded as the saving grace for an already decaying town due to the exodus of the whaling industry:

> Lahaina has too often been described to need a repetition here. Suffice it to say that voyagers are always glad to step ashore from the small schooners, and from the parching sun encountered on the deck, enjoy the cool sea-breeze that perpetually fans the town. To an occasional visitor, Lahaina grows older, and is putting on her gray hairs; her houses wear a rustier, gloomier look, her dobie walls are melting slowly away, fences fare hard, and even that which surrounds the 'City Hall,' the pride of the second city of Hawaii, is so dilapidated as to be a disgrace to the town if not to the government. And yet, for all that, one can see improvement even under the dusty robe that she always wears.

> The green that covers and surrounds her seems to grown (sic) more green, with fields extending to the right and left and up the hill-sides, wherever cane will grow. Sugar cane is the salvation of Lahaina, and to its cultivation, a large portion of the soil and of the inhabitants is now devoted. We have not heard any estimate of the area under cultivation, but should judge it to be not far from 1000 acres. It grows here most luxuriantly, yielding when well cultivated three and four tons of sugar to the acre. To grind this growing crop two mills have been erected, of which we shall notice first.[25]

Sugar was to be the savior from whaling, which had played a massive role in Lahaina and Hawai'i's socio-economic past. Lahaina was the capitol of the islands and a busy port town during the growth of this industry. Over the next 100 years or so, the industry of the town went from whaling to sugar cane, and then to tourism. At all times, then, the town was economically dependent on outside resources and multi-national entities. This in turn created a local oligarchy aligned with international demands. This dependent relationship is still at the root of social disparities today—one that continues to ensure economic inequality in the tourism industry. In Lahaina, though, the whaling and sugar industry growth narratives are represented as mostly positive. Artifacts of these eras are actively displayed

25 Henry M. Whitney, "Rural Sketches of the Hawaiian Islands, Lahaina Revisited," *The Pacific Commercial Advertiser*, March 26, 1864, 1.

and constantly referred to in contemporary Lahaina tourism discourse.

The following photos of Lahaina town and the surrounding areas are taken from the early 1900s, and show the more rural beginnings of this town.

Lahaina Street; Lahaina, Maui, Hawaii. ca. 1900. Courtesy of Bishop Museum

Front Street, Lahaina, Maui, Hawaii. Courtesy of Bishop Museum

Lahaina cane fields; Lahaina, Maui, Hawaii. Early 1900s. Courtesy of Bishop Museum

Coconut-frond fishing hut; Lahaina, Maui, Hawaii. 1908. Photo by Ray Jerome Baker. Courtesy of Bishop Museum

Up north from Lahaina is Ka'anapali. Prior to the land divisions that codified contemporary districts, Ka'anapali was a separate district that stretched from Keka'a point and Honokowai to the Ili o Kukuipuka, where Kahakuloa meets Wailuku. Taking in the entire back part of the West Maui Mountains, this area is a large, diverse, and culturally important region for the island of Maui.[26] At the top of Mauna Kahalawai, the West Maui Mountains, stands the summit Pu'u Kukui, reaching 5,788 feet above sea level.[27] Today known as the Pu'u Kukui Watershed Preserve, at "8,304 acres [it is] the largest private preserve in Hawai'i."[28] The rain from Pu'u Kukui flows into the Honokōhau Stream, and a waterfall measuring 1,700 feet sits at the base of the stream at Honokōhau Valley.[29] Many miles ma kai (to the sea) of this area is the Honolua-Mokulē'ia Marine Life Conservation District.[30] This geography is recorded in Sterling's *Sites of Maui*:

> Honokahau Falls and Kapalua Beach are on West Maui. The falls are in Honokahau Valley, dropping 1,120 feet in a horizontal distance of 500 feet, and have never been named before. Kapalua Beach is north of Napili Bay and has been known as Fleming or Fleming's Beach.[31]

---

26 Sterling, Kaanapali Map, 46.

27 Fujii, 15.

28 Fujii, 30.

29 Fujii, (from Kyselka and Lanterman, *Maui: How It Came to Be*, 62), 29.

30 Fujii, 15.

31 Sterling ("New Names for 4 Isle Waterfalls," *The Honolulu Advertiser*, Oct. 1, 1969, D4), 47.

The northernmost sections of West Maui are still not crossable in places, except via horse and by foot, because they are set against the sheer cliffs and valleys of Kahakuloa. As this area is still one of the least traveled areas on Maui, it contains many intact taro terraces, heiau, and wahi pana (sacred sites). W.M. Walker writes this about the historic Kihapi'ilani Trail that connects this area:

> The north end of West Maui also is traversed by a paved trail. Sections of it can be seen from Honolua to Honokohau and Kahakuloa. It is paved with beach rocks and has a width of four to six feet. Disregarding elevations and depressions it takes the shortest route between two points that is possible for foot travel. This trail is also spoken of as the Kihapiilani Trail. [32]

The Kihapiilani Trail is named after Kiha-a-Pi'ilani, the son of Pi'ilani. Kiha-a-Pi'ilani completed the construction on the trails started by his father. Pi'ilani had previously built "the alaloa, 'long road,' also called Alanui Kīke'eke'e-a-Maui, the King's Highway."[33] These roads crisscrossed the island of Maui and were built as a highway big enough "to accommodate eight of the king's warriors side by side."[34] These roads aided in trade and helped to unite the island under Pi'ilani and Kihapi'ilani's rule.

---

32 Sterling (W.M. Walker, *Archaeology of Maui*, 301), 46.

33 Fujii, (from personal interview with Edna Pualani Farden Bekeart on September 26, 2007 with Fujii), 17.

34 Fujii, 17-18.

In the northern region of the Lahaina district, Honokohau and Kahakuloa were also sites of vast taro and sweet potato cultivation and fishing ko'a (shrines).

> In all three valleys which you mention—Honokōwai, Honokohua and Honolua, as well as Kahana, there was considerable taro raised in olden times; as a matter of fact, a great deal was raised in Honokowai, where there must have been 30 or 40 acres under cultivation at one time. A detailed map of the kuleanas in that valley is available, and a fairly accurate estimate of the area could be made from that.[35]

Salt was also gathered at Kahana and as with Lahaina, many heiau stood in this area but have since been destroyed. There is also evidence of a holua site for the ali'i sport of sliding down the mountain on a board in Honolua.

Important heiau are Ili'ilikea Heiau and Maiu Heiau. Both were significant heiau of Kapalua Nui (the larger Kapalua area). Also present in this northern region is the Honokahua Preservation Site. The Ritz-Carlton Maui was originally to be built here, but was later moved because of the over 1,000 iwi kūpuna (ancestral bones) found during the excavation for the building of the hotel in 1998.[36] After massive public outcry led by the group Hui Alanui O Makena, the bones were repatriated and

---

35 Sterling (E.S.C. Handy, *Hawaiian Planter*, 106), 46.

36 Fujii, (from Theresa K. Donham and Paul H. Resenthal, "Data Recovery Excavations at the Honokahua Burial Site, Land of Honokahua, Lahaina District, Island of Maui," Prepared for Kapalua Land Company, Ltd., Hilo, Hawai'i, 2000, 8.1), 21.

the Native Hawaiian burial councils were created to supervise excavations statewide.[37]

Just up the coast is Honolua Bay. Honolua Bay was the last bit of land that Hōkūle'a, the Hawaiian Voyaging Canoe, left behind on her maiden voyage to Tahiti in 1976. As quoted in the book *Kapalua Nui*:

> 'Why Honolua?' pondered Herb Kawainui Kāne, a founder of the Polynesian Voyaging Society and the designer and builder of the double-hulled canoe. 'We felt that, from Honolua Bay and up around the north side of the island, we could pick winds that would carry the canoe away from land—clean, clear air without a lot of disruptions caused by the presence of land. Good, straight trade winds: sailing air. The cove from which Hōkule'a departed offered protection from winds and surf, and after clearing the point, the canoe caught the Northeast Tradewinds and was on its way.[38]

37 Fujii, 22.

38 Fujii, 51.

Kaanapali Landing; Kaanapali, Maui, Hawaii. ca. 1930. Unknown photographer, Inter-Island Airways. Courtesy of Bishop Museum

Inland view from Puu Kekaa (Black Rock) at start of development of Kaanapali, Maui, Hawaii. Photo five in a series of five. 1960. Courtesy of Bishop Museum

Culturally significant in numerous ways, the ʻāina north of Lahaina town maintains its mana (power) and cultural continuity.

Narrowing down the entire Lahaina District to a study of Kaʻanapali and Kekaʻa—today known as North Beach—is the purpose of this book. Of enormous cultural significance, the larger Kekaʻa area was at one time the capital of Hawaiʻi:

> Kaanapali has a proud heritage.... Before 1802, in the time of King Kekaalanao [Kekaalaneo], Kekaa was the name given to the site of the original capital of the islands which now make up the state of Hawaii. Kaanapali was the name given to the surrounding area.[39]

The following passage sheds more light on Kekaʻa:

> Kekaa was the capital of Maui when Kakaalaneo was reigning over West Maui... Many houses were constructed and people cultivated a great deal of potatoes, bananas, sugarcane, and things of a like nature. I have been told that the country now covered by cactus, in a northwesterly direction from Lahaina—was all cultivated. This chief (Kakaalaneo) also planted breadfruit and kukui trees down at Lahaina. Some of these trees southwest of the Lahaina fort, were called the bread fruit trees of Kauheana.[40]

---

39 Sterling (Jeanne Booth Johnson, "Ancient Land," *The Honolulu Advertiser* Hawaiian Holiday, Aug. 30, 1959, 15), 48.

40 Sterling (A. Fornander, *Collection*, 5:540-541 in E.S.C. Handy, *Hawaiian Planter*, 104-106), 37.

Keka'a is also the specific name of the cliff Pu'u Keka'a (hill of rumble thunder) at the tip of Ka'anapali. Pu'u Keka'a also means the "turning point hill."[41] This pu'u is located where the Sheraton Maui sits today and is known as Black Rock. A nightly reenactment of cliff diving here depicts the bravery of Ali'i who once dove off the cliff. Kahekili, the last great Maui chief, was known as a lele kawa (one who leaps feet first from high sea cliffs into the ocean). He made his jumps from Pu'u Keka'a. "Only someone with tremendous mana could jump and return unharmed from where the soul of the dead leapt over into the other world."[42] A prominent heiau to represent its importance was located at the top of this pu'u many generations before the building of the Sheraton Maui.

Historically, Kaululā'au was born at Keka'a. He was the son of Kaka'ālāneo, and was exiled to Lāna'i for cutting down breadfruit trees. He came back home after he "fought and overcame all the ghosts that made that island uninhabitable."[43] The many Ali'i from this area, and their battles, are also well documented. Many battles were fought here because of the proximity for warriors who would die by this leina a ka 'uhane. Death was reported to be frequent at Keka'a, and so this area was regarded as "ghostly." There are stories of people going from Ka'anapali to Lahaina and

41 Van James, 42.

42 Van James, 42.

43 Van James, 41.

seeing stones rolling down the hill from Keka'a—they explained, "Kekaa is ghostly! Kekaa is ghostly!"

> It is called a Leina-a-ka-uhane—the leaping place of the souls. Only the spirits of subjects (makaainana) go to Kekaa; the souls of farmers(fn) and the souls of chiefs go to the volcano when they die. If they have friends there some of them are driven back [*whenever they reenter the body*] and live again. [44]

There are other wahi pana in this area that are located ma uka (to the mountains) of the property of the Sheraton Maui. Two pōhaku (rocks) in particular are attached to mo'olelo—Pōhaku Moemoe and Pōhaku Wahine Pe'e. Maui the akua (god) started many of his adventures from Keka'a. Moemoe was Maui's tired and sleeping companion. Maui turned Moemoe to stone when he returned from slowing down the sun because Moemoe doubted Maui's ability to slow the sun and wouldn't help him.[45]

Pōhaku Wahine Pe'e is the "hiding woman." An 'aumakua who took the form of the owl, "She lived with other spirits in a cave called Ke Ana Pueo (the Owl Cave), located on the third and fourth holes of the Royal Kā'anapali Golf Course."[46] The first mo'olelo for this pōhaku is that a boy named Kāi'ili was

44 Sterling (A. Fornander, *Collection*, 5:542), 47. "(fn) Nowhere else is the idea presented of the souls of the lopa—the low farming class—being admitted to the same realm as those of the chiefs. On the contrary, lacking aumakuas to aid them, their spirits were doomed to a wondering friendless sphere."

45 Van James, 43.

46 Van James, 44.

kidnapped by warriors and was to be sacrificed at Haluluko‘ako‘a Heiau in Lahaina. His sister Nā‘ilima called for help at the cave and Wahine Pe‘e freed him and told him to walk backwards to Pu‘u Keka‘a so that the warriors could not track him.[47] The second mo‘olelo is that Wahine Pe‘e was also known as Pōhaku o Wahine o Manua for a woman who ran away from her abusive husband. She hid at the Haluluko‘ako‘a Heiau even though this heiau was kapu (forbidden) for women. An owl ‘aumakua led her to Pu‘u Keka‘a where she slept until morning and when she awoke she left Lahaina.[48] The stone looks like an owl head and is named for this ‘aumakua:

> Halulukoakoa, a coral structure, is famed traditionally as having given shelter to Wahine o Manua, a very beautiful young woman who fled from her husband in consequence of constant ill treatment. Regardless of the rigid kapu of the heiaus against women being allowed within their sacred walls, she hid herself therein and watched those searching for her. On their departure she ventured forth and on reaching the road an owl god appeared to her as guardian and guide, and led the pursued girl by the clapping of its wings, thru the brush till she reached the large stone mauka of Kekaa, Kaanapali (this is the hill against which the Sheraton-Maui is built) where it left her and she lay down

47 Van James, 44.

48 Van James, 44.

and slept till morn, when she arose and departed. The stone is now known as Pohaku o Manua."[49]

These wahi pana are marked today with plaques and stone boundaries, but one would not notice if not looking for them because they are incorporated into the golf courses at Ka'anapali.

Before contemporary Ka'anapali was constructed, sugar cane cultivation and a small airport occupied these areas. The Ka'anapali Airport was built in 1961 "to transport workers and materials into Amfac's new resort developed by Amfac inc."[50] Royal Hawaiian Air Service flew in and out of the airstrip located at North Beach (Keka'a). This runway ran adjacent to the beach and almost touched the shore. It was in existence until the early 1980s and some area locals still refer to this beach as "Airport Beach." The following photos depict the open vistas of the Ka'anapali area prior to, and during the massive construction of this area.

---

49 Sterling ([Wailehua Heaiau at Makila, Polanui, Lahaina—Walker Site 6] from J.F. McConkey, *The Maui News*, Oct. 18, 1969, 14), 50.

50 Paul Freeman, "Abandoned and little known airfields: Hawaii, Maui Island," Http://airfileds-freeman.com/HI/Airfields_HI_Maui.htm, 2001, 1.

Kaanapali Beach with a view toward Puu Kekaa (Black Rock) before development; Kaanapali, Maui, Hawaii. September 16, 1960. Courtesy of Bishop Museum

Maui Surf hotel; Kaanapali, Maui, Hawaii. March 1972. Courtesy of Bishop Museum

Kaanapali at the beginning of development; Kaanapali, Maui, Hawaii. September 16, 1960.
Courtesy of Bishop Museum

Inland view from Puu Kekaa (Black Rock) at start of development of Kaanapali, Maui, Hawaii. Photo four in a series of five. 1960. Courtesy of Bishop Museum

West Maui is beautiful, but it has also been transformed in ways not aligned to its natural beauty. From ahupuaʻa and wahi pana (sacred sites) to hotels, condominiums, and contested areas—the subdivision known as North Beach reflects all of these dynamics. The key to understanding the proverbial "here to there" in land tenure lies with understanding the roles played and the power employed by Pioneer Mill in this region for over a century. Pioneer Mill was the large landowner in Lahaina and Kaʻanapali in the early 1900s, and it maintained a criss-cross grid of domination over the economy and the people. Pineapple cultivation took over the more northern region of Honokahua and Honolua because of Honolua Ranch, later renamed Baldwin Packers in 1920 after operations were moved to Mālā Wharf.[51] Pioneer Mill even became a major player in pineapple, since "The sugar cane trains of Pioneer Mill transported Honolua pineapples to the new cannery, and the old cannery in Honokahua closed."[52] As for Kekaʻa, sugar cane production controlled land and water rights for the entire area. It is here that Pioneer Mill had the important role of not only producing industry, but also of shaping the land and citizens of Kekaʻa and the entire district.

---

51 Fujii (from Maui Land & Pineapple Company records), 59.

52 Fujii (from Rita Goldman, "Embracing the Past," *Embrace* (Kapalua), 2005, 32), 59.

Chapter 2: Pioneer Mill—Sugar King

Endless fields of sugar cane surrounded us when growing up on Maui and informed the local narrative. Sugar governed the lives of so many, and the view itself became the natural order of island life. The burning of the vast green cane fields to charred remnants, the hauling of the cane to the factories, and the stories from the plantation—both from the laborers who had no other choice but to work there and depend on the income for simple survival, or from those sent there to work for only a summer or two by their well-off parents so they might learn humility and appreciate hard work—were all experiences shared by those who worked in the cane fields, and these narratives were woven into the fabric of life on Maui.

But upon closer look, the structures that supported the fields of swaying cane are anything but natural. They instead symbolize darker narratives of land and power on Maui. Although waning now in economic importance to tourism, sugar acted as a dominating factor for land division and livelihood on Maui for many years, mostly visible through the layers of land transfers and water diversions that made this industry possible for over a century. Here the natural order gave way to the flexing of a powerful industry, one that controlled both the natural and social environment as plainly as the train tracks that once tirelessly transported the cane along the coast at Kaʻanapali.

Pioneer Mill began operations in 1863, and was a dominant sugar producer in Hawai'i until it closed operations in 1999. James Campbell and Henry Turton, in partnership with Benjamin Pitman, established Pioneer Mill on land once occupied by the Lahaina Sugar Company.[53] "By 1874, Campbell and Turton added the Lahaina Sugar Company and the West Maui Sugar Company, a venture of Kamehameha V, to the holdings of Pioneer Mill Company,"[54] In June 1877, followed by a July 1880 Agreement, Turton bought out Campbell's share of the property for $200,000 on a $250,000 loan that he received from Hackfield & Co.[55]

In the next few years, Turton continued to borrow money from Hackfield & Co. in order to develop the plantation and

---

53 William H. Dorrance, *Sugar Islands: The 165-year Story of Sugar in Hawai'i.* (Honolulu: Mutual Publishing, 2000), 63.

54 *Register of the Pioneer Mill Company Lahaina, Maui, 1873-1960*, "Pioneer Company History," Hawaiian Sugar Planters' Association Plantation (HSPA) Archives, University of Hawai'i, Mānoa, 1.

55 Mortgage, Henry Turton to James Campbell, June 16, 1877, Vol. 51, Page 24. Abstract of Title of Pioneer Mill Co. Ltd., In and To Lands of Puou, Euholilea, Kuhua, and Others, Lahiana, Maui, Land Court, Honolulu, Hawai'i, 129 & Agreement, H. Hackfield & Co. And H. Turton with James Campbell, July 19, 1880, Book 66, Page 151, Abstract of Title of Pioneer Mill Co. Ltd., In and To Lands of Puou, Euholilea, Kuhua, and Others, Lahiana, Maui, Land Court, Honolulu, Hawai'i, 132.

install the railroad system, for a debt totaling $431,483 plus 8% interest.[56] Campbell and Paul Isenberg then paid $100,000 on the first of the promissory notes (eleven in total) owed by Turton, thereby conveying Campbell and Isenberg interest in the property.[57] Turton then declared bankruptcy, and his interest in the property was revoked. He was stripped of ownership, and instead given the job of the plantation manager, with a pay of $200 a month. Henry Turton's obituary on July 11, 1887 briefly describes this dramatic reversal of fortune:

> [Tuton] bought out Mr. Campbell's interest in the plantation. The whole estate, with improvements, etc., were valued at $1,000,000.00. Shortly after this transaction, through the depreciation of real estate values and the decline of the sugar market, and supporting a large debt at high interest, the plantation proved too heavy a burden and the owner lost all he had gained through years of continual application.

Shedding a bit more light on Turton the person, the obituary continued:

> Of an exceptionally genial and friendly disposition, Mr. Turton was well liked by all who knew him, and having been one of the oldest foreign residents in the Kingdom, as well as one of the

---

56 Mortgage Deed, H. Turton to H. Hackfield. Bureau of Conveyances, Book 86, Page 244-258, 245-246.

57 Agreement, Paul Isenberg & H. Hackfield & Co., to James Campbell, July 23, 1884, Book 90, Page, 332. Abstract of Title of Pioneer Mill Co. Ltd., In and To Lands of Puou, Euholilea, Kuhua, and Others, Lahiana, Maui, Land Court, Honolulu, Hawai'i.

> most prominent figures in its industrial enterprises, his death is as the removal of an old landmark and leaves a large blank in our insular community. [58]

The company history narrative further records that in 1889, Campbell sold his interests to Horner (the next plantation manager), and Horner and Isenberg "incorporated Pioneer Mill Company on June 29, 1895."[59] Then "In 1918, Horner sold his interest to American Factors."[60] Hackfield & Co. was renamed American Factors (Amfac) to prove American patriotism from this German owned company in the midst of World War I. This somewhat tumultuous early history of Amfac gave way to the enormous growth of the plantation in the next century.

Over the years, and especially in the early 1900s, sugar cane production increased exponentially. And the water rights and land tenure—much of it leased and not owned—would impact West Maui for more than 100 years. Today, the land and water are still controlled by industry—now in the form of tourism. In fact, tourism was the predetermined inheritor of the sugar industry. This overview of Pioneer Mill and sugar in Hawai'i and Maui explains both the backdrop and forefront for the current land and water use for areas of West Maui, and specifically speaks to Pioneer Mill's control of Ka'anapali and North Beach.

---

58 "Obituary, Death of Henry Turton, Sr.," *The Daily Herald*, Honolulu, Hawaiian Islands, July 11, 1887.

59 "Pioneer Company History," 1.

60 "Pioneer Company History," 1.

Sugarcane field; West Maui, Hawaii. ca. 1945. Photo by Herbert Bauer. Courtesy of Bishop Museum

"Burning for Harvesting" Burning sugarcane before harvesting; Hawaii. ca. 1925. Photo by Williams Studio. Courtesy of Bishop Museum

"20 Young cane - Lahaina." Coconut trees growing among sugarcane; Lahaina, Maui, ca. 1912.
Courtesy of Bishop Museum

Sugar cane production began as a dominant environmental, social, political, and economic force in Hawai'i in the mid 1800s. The "Big Five" sugar plantation owners—Alexander & Baldwin Inc., Hackfield & Co. (Amfac, Inc.), C. Brewer & Co. Ltd., Theo H. Davies Co. Ltd., and Castle & Cooke—controlled just about every aspect of life in Hawai'i for over a century. The "interlocking directorates" and "corporate musical chairs" of the Big Five created a hierarchy that concentrated economic and political power in the hands of just a small number of individuals and corporations.[61] This influence intervened in Hawaiian sovereign territory because of the planters' political and economic influence and alliance with the United States during both the Hawaiian Kingdom and Territorial Government. They managed the violent merger of the Hawaiian Kingdom with the United States so that Hawaiian sugar was assured duty-free access to American markets. Sugar indeed became "King in Hawai'i" over a century ago, and in the ensuing years this industry has had a far-reaching impact because of this dominance.

"The Royal Hawaiian Agricultural Society was organized in August of 1850,"[62] and Dorrance notes that, "The years before 1850 were especially difficult because all land was owned by the Hawaiian Kingdom."[63] After the Mahele, land was opened for

61 Noel J. Kent, *Hawai'i: Islands Under the Influence.* (Honolulu: University of Hawai'i Press, [1983] 1993).

62 Dorrance, 13.

63 Dorrance, 11.

ownership and investment, which primarily helped to facilitate the sugar industry. With regard to Maui, Dorrance writes that:

> After deep wells and large-scale irrigation ditches were introduced, Maui blossomed as a major sugar producer. As on the other islands, before irrigation its plantations were small and concentrated in the wettest areas. Over the years Maui managed to increase its share of Hawai'i's sugar production despite the inroads of urban and resort development. [64]

In 1850, Hawai'i exported 375 tons of sugar. This amount was drastically reduced to 11 tons of sugar the following year, mostly because California was admitted to the Union and tariffs were enforced on Hawaiian sugar.[65] In the next 20 years, massive growth of this industry facilitated economic and political power for the Big 5. After the Civil War ended in America, and the North and South were once again trading, the Hawai'i sugar planters anticipated a loss of revenue. Therefore, the sugar plantation owners favored the passage of the Reciprocity Treaty in 1876. This treaty assured that Hawai'i's sugar would be admitted to the Union tariff-free. The Bayonet Constitution then sealed the deal with the ceding of the Pearl Harbor Estuary to the United States, allowing for the continued free flow of sugar between the two countries. The Planters Convention (1882) and the implementation of the Hawaiian Sugar Planters' Association

64 Dorrance, 60.

65 Dorrance, 152.

(1895) further organized this industry, and only fairly recently, in 1996, when the HSPA's representative and staff in Washington D.C. disbanded.[66]

Pioneer Mill played a major role in this all-encompassing industry: "In 1885, Pioneer Mill Company was cultivating 600 of the 900 acres owned by the company and by 1910, 8,000 acres were devoted to growing cane."[67] According to the Balance Sheets of the Company, in 1923 Pioneer Mill had 8,341.94 acres under cultivation, the total assets of the company were $11,818,775.57, and 222,018.69 tons of sugar cane cultivated, which in turn produced a net profit for the company of $1,023,537.07.[68] In the early 1900s, the profits remained fairly consistent, with some variance due to weather impacts and subtractions because of the substantial amount of money that went to water diversions and for other maintenance of the plantation. In 1935, though, signs of the Depression were apparent. The total assets of the company were $8,659,369.83, and 374,198.31 tons of sugar cane were produced, for a net profit of $723,942.85.[69]

The Balance Sheets of the company relate this information in simple ledgers, but the Pioneer Mill Manager's Reports from the early 1900s shed a bit more light on the finances and the growth desires of the company. For instance, the Manager's

---

66 Dorrance, 153 & 155.

67 "Pioneer Company History," 1.

68 "Balance Sheets, Annual 1916-1935," 0-1-4 PMC, HSPA Archives, Hamilton Library, University of Hawai'i, Mānoa.

69 "Balance Sheets, Annual 1916-1935," HSPA Archives.

Report for the year ending December 31, 1901 identifies the primary concerns for the company as water, railroad, and land acquisitions:

> The following permanent improvements have been made, necessitating an outlay of about $640,000.00.
>
> 1st Construction of eight reservoirs for the storage of regular pump and mountain water, and for the gathering of occasional freshets. Of these reservoirs, three are situated at Lahaina proper, four at Kaanapali and one (just completed) at Wahikuli, directly above the crater Laiua. This crater is a natural reservoir and will also be used hereafter in case of heavy freshets. The great advantage of having these reservoirs is the abandonment of expensive and inefficient night irrigation, also a substantial saving of pumping expenses.
>
> 2nd Construction of twenty miles of permanent railroad, replacing part of the old track, and extending from one end of the plantation to the other, with branch lines to higher elevations. This road, together with three miles of old and seven miles of newly acquired portable track, enables us to take off our crops in good season and to the best advantage for the growing of rations.
>
> 3rd Acquirement of one new Baldwin locomotive and 145 cane cars.
>
> Your Directors have just concluded an agreement with Hon. H.P. Baldwin, by which the Company will acquire an additional amount of eight to twelve million gallons of mountain water per day from the Honokohau Gulch; this agreement will be submitted for your approval.

The Treasurer's Report noted 150,785 bags, 8,959.430 net

tons, and $592,292.09 net proceeds of sugar for Pioneer Mill in 1901.[70]

In 1901, a budding water conversation was already showing signs of completely dominating the discourse, an obsession that continued to escalate over the years. The Manager's Report for 1903 exemplified this:

> Prospecting for water by tunneling in the mountains has been continued and proves to be a profitable investment. The water supply has been increased during the year by about three million gallons, making a total of seven and one-half million gallons of mountain water derived from three different sources.
>
> The total expenditure for this quantity of water is $21,485.42, or $2860 per million gallons. Taking as a base the rent to be paid for the Honokahau water, $3,000.00 per one million gallons per year, our own supply developed by tunneling, would represent a value of $338,400.00. The prospects for a further increase during the coming year are excellent.
>
> Expenditures for permanent improvements during the coming year will include flumes, ditches and reservoirs for about 1,000 acres of new land. This will nearly take in the balance of all of the available cane land, bringing the total acreage of the plantation under cultivation to about 6,000 acres.
>
> The Honokahau Ditch is almost ready for the water. Scarcity

---

70 "Report of the Pioneer Mill Co. Ltd. for Fifteen Months Ending December 31, 1901," Hawn Hd 9109.P56A37, HSPA Archives, Hamilton Library, University of Hawai'i, Mānoa.

> of labor, rain and other unforeseen complications have delayed its completion beyond all expectations. [71]

The Honokohau Ditch was completed in 1904. This ditch had a capacity of carrying up to 30 million gallons of water, and was supported with nine reservoirs just below the elevation, designated to store up to 70 million gallons of water.[72] By 1909, a new reservoir was instituted at Ka'anapali, with a capacity of 11,000,000 gallons of water. That annual report noted, "We are continuing to develop water, and during the past year we have secured an additional supply of 1,000,000 gallons,"[73] and the 1910 report indicated that "The largest part of money for improvements has been spent on developing, storing, and controlling the water."[74]

Controlling the water was key for Pioneer Mill, and the diversion of water from the northern to the southern parts of the Lahaina district was its primary initiative in the early 1900s:

> A ditch, flume and siphon have been constructed through the Kahoma and Kanaha Gulches, which enable us to take the

---

71 "Report of the Pioneer Mill Co. Ltd. for Fifteen Months Ending December 31, 1903," HSPA Archives.

72 "Report of the Pioneer Mill Co. Ltd. for Fifteen Months Ending December 31, 1904," HSPA Archives.

73 "Report of the Pioneer Mill Co. Ltd. for Fifteen Months Ending December 31, 1909," HSPA Archives.

74 "Report of the Pioneer Mill Co. Ltd. for Fifteen Months Ending December 31, 1910," HSPA Archives.

> Honokahau, Honokawai and Wahikuli waters over to the Lahaina section of the plantation, thus relieving the Lahaina pumps. [75]

In the following year the report indicates that "The syphons, flumes and ditches bringing the Honokahau and Honokawai surplus water to the Lahaina side, have been in operation since April, and have given great satisfaction." [76]

As for other overall improvements:

> Electrical power has been brought down to the wharf at Kaanapali. The piling of sugar is done by two Brown stackers. A new scow has been built, so that we now have four in all. A new boiler has been installed. Our shipping facilities are good, and the landing and warehouses are in splendid condition. [77]

The plantation was growing, due in large part to the diversion of water. This enabled vast cane fields to stretch across the very dry southern part of the district. An agreement was struck in 1915 for a new lease between Pioneer Mill and H.P. Baldwin. This lease would be in effect for 15 years and directed the building of a new ditch to store an additional 50 million gallons of water. In addition:

---

75 "Report of the Pioneer Mill Co. Ltd. for Fifteen Months Ending December 31, 1910," HSPA Archives.

76 "Report of the Pioneer Mill Co. Ltd. for Fifteen Months Ending December 31, 1911," HSPA Archives.

77 "Report of the Pioneer Mill Co. Ltd. for Fifteen Months Ending December 31, 1911," HSPA Archives.

> The Government has renewed the old Honokowai lease for a term of fifteen years. The old lease expired April, 1912. One new reservoir, with a capacity of six million gallons, is under construction on the Honokowai section and will be finished about March, 1913. One old reservoir at Kauaula has been enlarged, adding six million gallons to the former capacity. At the present time we are enlarging the Wahikuli reservoir to hold an additional quantity of twenty million gallons. [78]

Cement linings to the ditches were introduced then, and in 1913:

> The new tunnels deliver the water into our old ditch at the same point on the north side of the Honokawai gulch from where the old ditch has been widened to carry 60 million gallons. Of the 50 million gallons 30 million can be brought over to the Lahaina section, enabling us to stop the pumps entirely during a year of average rainfall. [79]

It was also during this time period when the United States began to take further notice of water resources in Hawai'i. The United States Geological Survey, Department of the Interior began a study "dating from July 1, 1910 for 'the gaging of streams and the determination of the water supply of the Territory of

78 "Report of the Pioneer Mill Co. Ltd. for Fifteen Months Ending December 31, 1912," HSPA Archives.

79 "Report of the Pioneer Mill Co. Ltd. for Fifteen Months Ending December 31, 1913," HSPA Archives.

Hawaii.'"[80] This study was spurred by an "Act to promote the conservation and development of the natural resources of the Territory," passed by the Legislature of the Territory of Hawaii on March 22, 1909.[81]

This Act established a conservation fund, one tied to immigration:

> A special tax of 2 per cent shall be levied, assessed, and collected annually on all incomes in excess of $4,000; and all amounts so collected shall constitute a special fund to be expended only for the encouragement of immigration and the conservation of natural resources in the proportion of three-fourths for immigration and one-fourth for conservation. The conservation fund shall be used for the development, conservation, improvement, and utilization of the natural resources and shall be available for expenditure at such times and in such manner as a board of three persons appointed in accordance with section 80 of the organic act shall, with the approval of the governor, determine. [82]

The goal of the U.S. Geological Survey was to locate and document the water resources of Hawai'i, and also to find new ways to encourage immigration for the industry. This survey found that "Sugar cane, by far the most important product, gives the largest yields on those lands where the proper amount of

80 W.F. Martin and C.H. Pierce, "Water Resources of Hawaii 1909-1911." Department of the Interior, United States Geological Survey, Washington Printing Office, 1913, 15.

81 Martin and Pierce, 12.

82 Martin and Pierce, 12.

water can be applied at the right time, and large areas planted in cane depend entirely on irrigation." The survey also noted that "Taro, which furnishes the staple food for a considerable part of the population, requires a continual application of water during its growth,"[83] but this one sentence was outweighed by the dominant sugar discourse. Sugar production overwhelmed this document, even though the loss of water for the development of this industry was warned against: "Losses of irrigation need to be continually guarded against in order to secure the maximum results from a supply that is definitely limited."[84]

This voracious appetite for water is well documented in Pioneer Mill's early Manager's Reports. In 1913, there were over 30 million gallons being pumped from the Honokowai gulch to Lahaina. In that same year, land leased from H.P. Baldwin to Pioneer Mill included "virgin land" of almost 700 acres below the Honokohau water system for cultivation.[85] In 1919, the rights to the water were further clarified:

> During the year an agreement was concluded with the trustees of the Estate of H.P. Baldwin, whereby the Company is enabled to take in an additional cane area of approximately 350 acres in Honokowai between the Alaeloa and Kahana gulches. The agreement also gives the Company the rights to water

83 Martin and Pierce, 15.

84 Martin and Pierce, 15-16.

85 "Report of the Pioneer Mill Co. Ltd. for Fifteen Months Ending December 31, 1913," HSPA Archives.

sources and the development thereof, thus adding materially to its water supply system. [86]

In each report, water is the primary concern, constituting the bread and butter of the plantation. It is in these early documents and plantation times that the entire system of water and land control was created—with the Honokohau Ditch providing the biggest source of mountain water for the entire plantation:

> Irrigation of Pioneer Mill Company's fields, an area approximately ten miles long and one and one half miles wide with altitudes between ten and 700 feet, was accomplished with water drawn from wells and water transported from the West Maui Mountains. The McCandless brothers drilled the first well on Maui for Pioneer Mill Company in 1883. By 1935, over $3,000,000 had been spent on water development, including gravity systems and underground supplies. [87]

The total operating costs for water increased exponentially after 1919, when the Honokohau ditch and water operations were listed at $34,578. By 1920 the number jumped to $85,931, and by 1925 the total operating costs at Honokohau was $102,638. The majority of the cost went to the lining of the ditches with cement, an endeavor that continued in earnest.[88] The maintenance of the ditch, which included days lost by

86 "Report of the Pioneer Mill Co. Ltd. for Fifteen Months Ending December 31, 1919," HSPA Archives.

87 "Pioneer Company History," 2.

88 "Honokohau Water Costs August 30, 1919-Sept. 30, 1928," PMC 0-1-6, HSPA Archives.

turning the water off, was counted as an operating cost. Besides water concerns, Pioneer Mill signed an agreement in 1919 with Baldwin Packers to deliver pineapple. The Pioneer Mill railroad was extended to Napili to haul pineapple from the cannery to the landing and shipping areas. This agreement was in effect for 32 years. [89]

The steam turbine introduced to plantation operations in 1918 ensured a more complete reliance on water. In a 1918 Manager's Report, where the obsession for water was continuously and monotonously spelled out, only one line mentioned the laborers' quarters: "Large improvements and repair work have been made in this connection (laborers' quarters), and 140 houses of various kind have been built."[90] In these early reports, the plantation laborers' quarters and camps are noted as needing and receiving some improvements and maintenance. However, the notation about the laborers' quarters were so typically brief, and appearing almost as an administrative afterthought.

> I think I was thirteen when I fist (sic) started working for the plantation. We were young, so they used to tell us, 'You work for the dairy. Truck will be waiting over here for you folks. Ride this truck and they'll take you to your working area.' At times, we used to go out and pick kiawe beans. We used to go out way

89 "Agreements, Miscellaneous," 1-2 PMC, HSPA Archives.

90 "Report of the Pioneer Mill Co. Ltd. for Fifteen Months Ending December 31, 1917," HSPA Archives.

> on the far end before you got to Wailuku. . . . There, they used to give us a bag and we used to get a box, fill up the box [with kiawe beans] and put it into the bag. They used to pay us by the pound. They paid us nine tenths of a cent, not one cent, nine tenths of a cent per pound. [91]

Stories from the plantation laborers themselves often relate the grueling work and harsh conditions experienced on the plantation. But the stories also tell of camaraderie and a sense of community continuity. Many of the people who came to Hawai'i to work on the sugar plantations in search of a better life stayed, and made a home for themselves and the generations to come. And in this diaspora, the plantation itself became the lifeline, serving as a mainstay for immigrant families working in Hawai'i. The plantation camps provided not just homes for the occupants, but also instituted an entire social structure so that work and home life were intertwined, effectively producing the local citizen worker.

Churches, dance halls, hospitals, transportation to sporting (football, baseball, track and field) and social events (the Maui Fair, dances), schools, theaters, etc., were all provided and maintained by the plantation, which took on the role of patriarchal father and community resource to its laborers, while also training an entire generation of disciplined factory workers:

---

91 Kazukiyo "Jiggs" Kuboyama, Biographical Summary. *Pioneer Mill Company: A Maui Sugar Plantation Legacy*. Center for Oral History, Social Science Research Institute, University of Hawai'i, Mānoa, December 2003.

> Although they knew that the plantation was in reality a factory in the fields and a capitalistic enterprise designed to earn profits, many managers viewed it as a social community, and they saw themselves as guardians responsible for the welfare of the workers. [92]

Ethnic pride, alongside the American work ethic, was the emotional by-product of these plantation communities. This orientation to citizenship still resonates in places in Hawai'i today, and the actual work structures and protocol systems of leadership that began on the plantation are still prominent in many work spaces for both state and non-state jobs. Here was the chance to structure an entire generation of workers, both on and off the fields. Here was the chance to create the citizen (American in concept, ethnic in actuality) and influence not only work life but home life as well.

The Pioneer Mill camp map shown below lists 22 camps carved out of the West Maui terrain. Some of these camps are described ethnically (Portuguese Camp, Filipino Camp), some are described geographically in terms of where they are on the plantation (Wahikuli Pump Camp, Lahaina Pump Camp), and others are described by names of families (Marayama Camp, Hirai Camp). Regardless of the names, all of these camps were entire communities and had distinct yet similar systems of operations.

---

92 Ronald Takaki, *Pau Hana: Plantation Life and Labor in Hawaii*. (Honolulu: University of Hawai'i Press, 1983), 60.

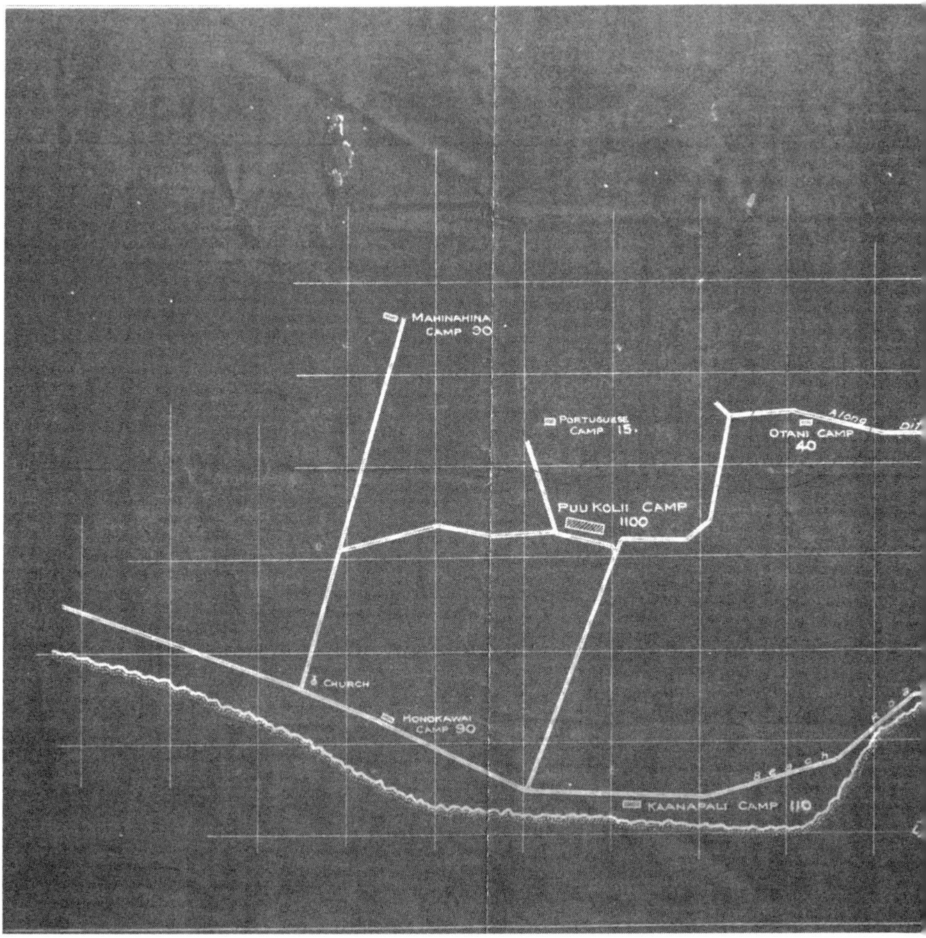

Pioneer Mill Company camps blueprints. Courtesy of Bishop Museum.

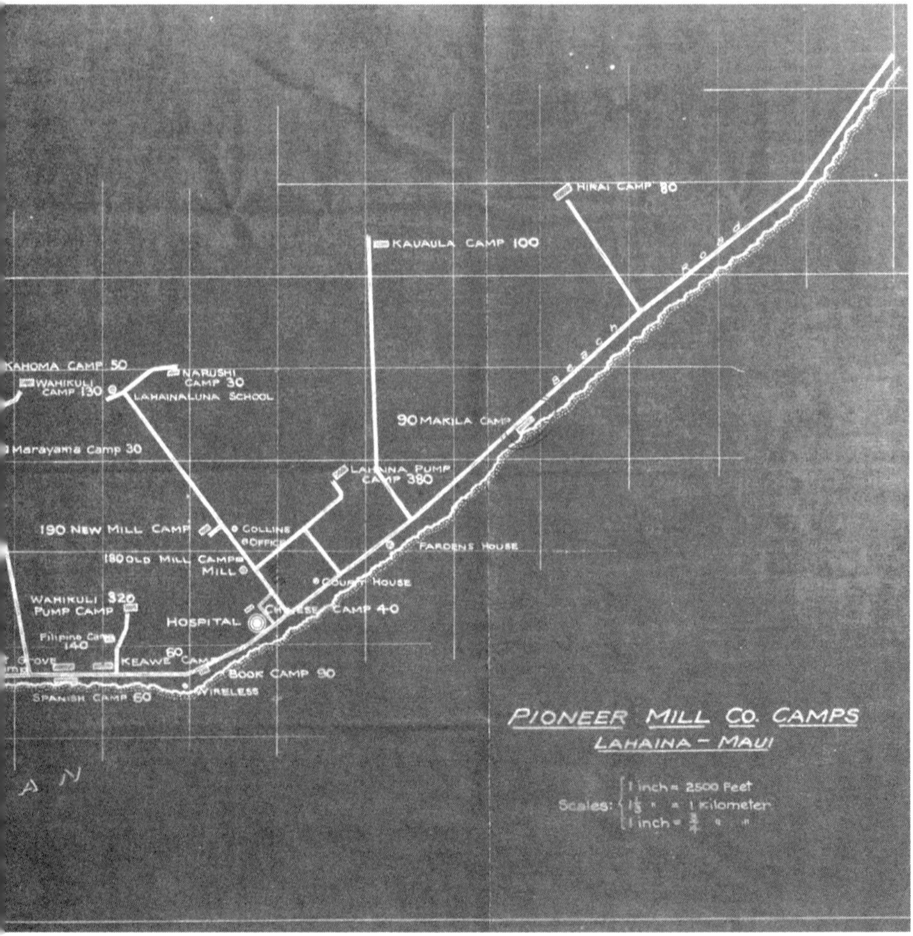
HIRAI CAMP 80
KAUAULA CAMP 100
Beach Road
KAHOMA CAMP 50
WAHIKULI CAMP 130
NARUSHI CAMP 30
LAHAINALUNA SCHOOL
90 MAKILA CAMP
Marayama Camp 30
LAHAINA PUMP CAMP 380
190 NEW MILL CAMP
COLLINS
OFFICE
FARDENS HOUSE
180 OLD MILL CAMP
MILL
COURT HOUSE
WAHIKULI 320 PUMP CAMP
HOSPITAL
CAMP 40
Filipino Camp 140
60 KEAWE
BOOK CAMP 90
WIRELESS
SPANISH CAMP 60
PIONEER MILL CO. CAMPS
LAHAINA – MAUI
Scales:
1 inch = 2500 Feet
1 Kilometer

In these communities, race, gender, and age dictated the movement of bodies at work and home. Ronald Takaki documents in *Pau Hana*, "Plantation authority was reinforced by an occupational structure that stratified plantation employment according to race."[93] The tracking of race was done precisely by the Hawaiian Sugar Planters Association and by the individual plantations because managers and planters depended on this structure for plantation survival. A statewide workforce based on ethnicity was recorded in The Hawaiian Sugar Planters Census Reports for 1927-1929:

Race	Citizens	Aliens	Total
Hawaiian	3,483		3,483
Caucasian	15,069	674	15,743
Chinese	898	458	1,356
Japanese	34,056	12,246	46,302
Koreans	564	512	1,076[94]

Another Census Report for 1937 and 1938 for Pioneer Mill summarized the workers according to ethnicity and earnings ($):

93 Takaki, 75.

94 "Census of Sugar Workers, HSPA 1927-1929, 1935-1941," 1-14 PMC, HSPA Archives.

Number of Employees	3,106
Payroll gross	473,435
Total Hawaiian Men	1,489,585
Hawaiian Women	73,515
Hawaiian Minors	169
Portuguese Men	963,710
Portuguese Minors	25,025
Puerto Ricans	76,075
Spanish	229,795
Chinese	129,705
Koreans	55,210
Filipino Men	73,741
Filipino Women	46,740
Filipino Minors	3,890
Japanese Minors	106,640
Japanese Women	757,770
Japanese Men	6,425,375
Men	12,774,035[95]

Census Reports for Pioneer Mill in 1939 recorded a total of 23,960 employees situated in just 4,963 houses island-wide.[96]

95 "Personnel & Payroll: Sept.-Dec. 1937 & 1938," 0-1-3 PMC, HSPA Archives.

96 "Maui Summary HSPA Census June 30, 1939," PMC, HSPA Archives.

The Census Report further numbered Filipino citizens at 9,930, all other citizens at 741, Filipino Aliens at 23,240, and all other aliens at 105—with a total of 63.5% Citizens and 36.5% Aliens. The overwhelming majority of workers in both categories were therefore Filipino.[97] The further breakdown reports for Pu'ukoli'i, located ma uka (mountain-side) of Ka'anapali, recorded this camp as the largest camp in West Maui. In the same year, Pioneer Mill also recorded the children workers as follows:

Japanese	5,590
Filipino	1,934
Chinese	158
Korean	118
Puerto Rican	482
Portuguese	1,361
Hawaiian	510
Anglo Saxon	167
All Others	195[98]

The workers were paid according to their ethnicity and the job performed. Adding to this structure was an interesting and alarming "cost comparison" done by the four Maui plantations to insure that none of them paid their laborers more than the

97 "Maui Summary HSPA Census June 30, 1939," HSPA Archives.

98 "Maui Summary HSPA Census June 30, 1939," HSPA Archives.

other plantations' wages. This "cost comparison" method was also used for items purchased—no plantation paid more for any one item than another plantation paid. This system helped the plantations maintain a lid on the expenses of the industry.

ADDRESS CORRESPONDENCE TO THE COMPANY

AGENTS
ALEXANDER & BALDWIN, LTD.
HONOLULU SAN FRANCISCO
SEATTLE

TELEGRAPHIC ADDRESS "COMMERCIAL"

HAWAIIAN COMMERCIAL AND SUGAR COMPANY
LIMITED

PUUNENE, MAUI, HAWAII.

November 15, 1932.

Mr. A. D. Gordon, Cashier,
Pioneer Mill Co., Ltd.
Lahaina, Maui.

Dear Arthur:

Thanks very much for your letter of the 14th instant showing certain mill costs. Since we all work the Repairs account differently, there is no doubt that it is better to leave this item out of the comparative report.

I have now completed a comparison of the four Maui plantations showing the factory costs and enclose copy of this statement herewith, and trust you may find same of interest.

In your memo you ask me how Puunene distributes the Mill Timekeeper's salary, and in reply would advise that his salary is charged direct to Superintendence during the operating season, and in the off season his time is charged direct to Mill Maintenance. As a matter of information, you will find below the various positions making up the item of Superintendence:

Mr. Lougher	-	Superintendent
Mr. Taylor	-	Engineer
Mr. Kiakona	-	Night Engineer
Mr. Glick	-	Head Chemist
Mr. Williams	-	Sugar Boiler
Mr. Du Bois	-	Timekeeper

Yours very truly,

FACTORY RATES

Mill for 2 Shifts	Max.	Min.	No. Men	Ave. Rate
HANDLING CANE				
Scalemen	$2.30	$2.10	2	$2.20
Unloading Machine	Contract		2	
Handling Cars	"		10	
CRUSHING CANE				
Mill Tender	2.30	2.10	2	2.20
Engine tenders	1.65	1.65	2	1.65
Oilers	1.50	1.25	6	1.34
Crusher Feeders	1.50	1.45	2	1.48
Juice Pan Men	1.25	1.20	4	1.23
BAGASSE				
Trashmen	1.20	1.20	10	1.20
STEAM				
Water tender	1.80	1.45	2	1.63
Firemen	2.00	1.20	11	1.63
Ashmen	1.45	1.20	4	1.30
Luna	2.30	2.10	2	2.20
ELECTRICIAN	1.55	1.55	1	1.55
POWERHOUSE OPERATORS	2.25	2.00	2	2.13

BOILING HOUSE:	Max.	Min.	No. Men	Ave. Rate
LABORATORY				
Assistant Chemists	$2.25	$2.25	2	$2.25
Sample boys	1.50	.65	5	1.18
CLARIFICATION				
Juice Scale	1.40	1.30	2	1.35
Lime Tender			1	1.25
Juice Heaters	1.30	1.20	2	1.25
Settlers	1.30	1.30	2	1.30
Luna	2.25	1.55	2	1.90
FILTRATION				
Presses	1.20	1.20	10	1.20
Repairs Cloth			1	.75
Lunas	1.40	1.40	2	1.40
EVAPORATION				
Evaporators	1.40	1.40	2	1.40
GRAINING				
Vacuum Pans	2.30	1.20	5	1.73
Crystallizers	2.20	1.85	2	2.08
Mixers	1.50	1.40	2	1.45
DRYING & BAGGING				
Cent. #1	1.45	1.40	10	1.41
Cent. #2	1.20	1.20	10	1.20
Cent. Luna	1.55	1.55	2	1.55
Oilers	1.60	1.50	2	1.55
Molasses Tender	2.65	1.50	2	2.08
Bagging, Weighing&Sewing	1.85	1.50	4	1.63
Loading on Cars	1.50	1.50	4	1.50
Sweeper	1.25	1.25	1	1.25

SUPERINTENDENCE	Max.	Min.	No. Men	Ave. Rate
Superintendence				
Engineer				
Watch Engineers				
Fireroom Foreman				
Boiling House Foreman				
Shift Sugar Boilers				
Chemist				
Timekeeper				

GENERAL REPAIR GANG

	Max.	Min.	No. Men	Ave. Rate
GENERAL REPAIR MEN	$2.25	$1.00	16	$1.58
MACHINE SHOP				
Foreman			1	
Machinists	2.70	1.45	8	1.90
Helpers	1.25	1.25	3	1.25
Welders	1.85	1.45	2	1.65
Toolroom man			1	1.50
BLACKSMITH SHOP				
Blacksmith				
Helpers	2.25	2.00	2	2.13
MASONS				
Masons	2.25	1.55	3	1.78
Helpers	1.45	1.25	2	1.35
BOILERMAKERS				
Boilermaker			1	
Assistants			6	1.98

COMPARISON HARVESTING COSTS PER TON CANE

1933 CROP TO FEBRUARY 28th, 1933

	HC&SCO.	MACO.	PMCO.	WSCO.
CUTTING CANE	.2475	.2129	.2335	.223
LOADING CANE	.3119	.2771	.2128	.265
HAULING CANE	.2683	.3367	.2557	.282
FLUMING CANE			.0903	
TOTAL COST PER TON HARVESTING	.8277	.8267	.7953	.773
Average Tons Cut Per Man per Day	5.285	6.6	6.98	8.80
Average Tons Loaded Per Man per Day: Machine	10.258	7.2		9.23
Hand			10.14	

AVERAGE DAILY EARNINGS ALL EMPLOYEES - YEAR 1932

Hawaiian Commercial & Sugar Co.,Ltd........$2.05 per Day

Maui Agricultural Co.,Ltd.................. 1.935 " "

Pioneer Mill Co.,Ltd.......................1.837 " "

Wailuku Sugar Company......................1.852 " "

STORE EMPLOYEES

Pioneer includes its Store Employees in its Labor Statistics. H.C.&S.Co.,Ltd. & M.A.Co.,Ltd. do not.

Puunene, Maui, T.H.,
March 29, 1933.

These cost comparison lists were closely tracked. Members from the four Maui plantations—Hawaiian Commercial & Sugar Co., Ltd., Maui Agricultural Co., Ltd., Pioneer Mill Co., Ltd., and Wailuku Sugar Co.—would meet every month over lunch to discuss wages and prices. A letter from 1932 shows a very causal communication between the heads of the four Maui sugar plantations:

Hawaiian Commercial and Sugar Company
Limited
Puunene, Maui, Hawaii
November 15, 1932

Messrs. A.D. Gordon,
Leslie Bisset
G.N. Weight

Gentlemen,

Enclosed please find a memo, in duplicate, covering certain mill work at the four Maui plantations, which I trust you may find of interest.

Yours very truly,
D.C. Rattray [99]

99 "Comparative Costs: Labor, 1930-1933," 1-16 PMC, HSPA Archives.

While "cost comparison" kept costs down, it also ensured that the laborers would not exceed their lot in life:

> Many planters had their own views of the future of Hawaii and the kind of society the islands should have. Generally they wanted to maintain the hierarchical social structure of the plantation—White over Asian and capitalist over laborer.[100]

Well into the 1980s, the *Pioneer Mill News Bulletin* showed how the production of the citizen-worker was carried out. As a community resource, the *Bulletin* provided work and home suggestions, gave the workers "words to ponder," and encouraged safety above all else so that a reliable work force was produced. Plantation paternalism was strongly exemplified in the Bulletin:

> Safety:
> We all hear about on-the-job safety, but have you given some thought of off-the-job safety? The same common sense rules that apply here at work also apply at home. For example:
> 1. Do you keep your housekeeping up to par? Keep combustible trash thrown away? Keep tripping and slipping hazards out of your house and yard?
> 2. How about your workshop or garage? Do you know how to safely use those power tools? Do you keep flammables such as gasoline in safety containers? Do you use safety glasses or goggles when working on those "do-it-yourself" projects?
> 3. How about fire safety? Do you have a small portable fire

100 Takaki, 158.

extinguisher of the right type for common household fires? Do you have a plan of action if there is a fire?

4. Do you have emergency telephone numbers (doctor, ambulance, police, and fire department) readily available in case of emergency? How about first aid?

Please think about off-the-job safety. Your life might depend on it. [101]

In each weekly newsletter, the "Words To Ponder" section was made up mostly of quotes for the workers to adapt as their own. Here is the July 9, 1979 installment.

- In the battle of life, talent is the punch; tact is the clever footwork.
- The world is full of willing people; some willing to work, the rest willing to let them.
- A man must be big enough to admit his mistakes, smart enough to profit from them, and strong enough to correct them. [102]

And to sum it up: "THINK! DON'T DREAM ON JOB. Everyone likes to dream. But let's not do it on the job. It's no good for you, your department, your plant, or your company." [103] The only elements missing here are "it's no good for your country, your family, or your life." After reading the News Bulletin, it is

101 *Pioneer Mill News Bulletin*, April 1976-October 1982. (inc.), April 4, 1979. Hamilton Library, University of Hawai'i, Mānoa.

102 *Pioneer Mill News Bulletin*, April 1976-October 1982. (inc.), July 9, 1979.

103 *Pioneer Mill News Bulletin*, April 1976-October 1982. (inc.), July 16, 1979

easy to comprehend just how the plantation took on the role of extended family, completely involved in its laborers' lives.

A primary concern for the company, as explained in the *Bulletin*, was the laborers' health. This concern was tied to factory production, because hurt laborers cost the plantation money. The Lost-Time Accidents section of the newsletter provided positive reinforcement to the workers for staying safe—both on and off the job. The February 14, 1980 *Newsletter* noted, "In 1979, we had 197 total accidents, 24 lost-time accidents, and 355 man-days lost. Our 1980 Safety Goal is a 35% reduction in all categories."[104] The following safety tip added:

> What Accidents Cost You
>
> We all know that accidents are expensive, but here are some comparisons that make costs more tangible. According to Vincent Tofany, President of the National Safety Council, if we could eliminate all work accidents, we could reward every wage earner with a $5 a week raise. If we could declare a moratorium on traffic accidents, we could finance a 29-cent rebate on every gallon of gasoline. If there were some way of doing away with home accidents, it would mean an additional $95 to every household in the United States. And if we could eliminate all accidents, we could give every individual income tax payer an $800 rebate.
>
> In 1978, accidents cost $68.7 billion in wage losses, medical and insurance costs, property damage in motor vehicle accidents, fire losses, and indirect losses from work accidents.

104 *Pioneer Mill News Bulletin*, April 1976-October 1982. (inc.), February 14, 1980.

From: Family Safety [105]

A Safety Incentive Program was instituted in 1981 at Pioneer Mill to help encourage on-the-job safety. The names of employees who managed to avoid injury were put into a drawing for "valuable prizes."[106] But accidents on the job actually increased during this year, so the program was extinguished, with the words "we will be re-evaluating the safety incentive program." [107]

To keep order, the administrative structure of the plantation was itself a heavily enforced top-down supervision and protocol system. A Pioneer Mill Industrial Relations Programming report says:

> In 1933, when the present manager of Pioneer Mill assumed responsibility for the operation of this organization, he analyzed his management group and its activities. He believed that in the final analysis the success of any enterprise depended upon the caliber of its key personnel—Supervision. [108]

The activities to be encouraged were:

1. Organizational structure.
2. Written policies and procedures.
3. Job descriptions and wage and salary administration.

---

105 *Pioneer Mill News Bulletin*, April 1976-October 1982. (inc.), October 7, 1980.

106 *Pioneer Mill News Bulletin*, April 1976-October 1982. (inc.), February 6, 1981.

107 *Pioneer Mill News Bulletin*, April 1976-October 1982. (inc.), September 19, 1981.

108 "Case Study No. 5, Industrial Relations Programming, Pioneer Mill Company, Ltd.," *Case Study of Effective Industrial Relations Case Study No. 1, Employee Information Program Hawaiian Pineapple Co., Ltd.* Honolulu, 1951, 1.

4. Work-performance ratings.
5. Training and communications. [109]

Under each subheading is a summary of how the managers should carry out these initiatives. This structure was put in place to encourage fear and deference to authority. Managers (lunas) were paid more. This established protocol also ensured a psychological distancing of the administration "to enhance the prestige of individual supervisors and make communications effective."[110] Hotels would create similar authority structures, as they became Hawai'i's next plantation. The Department of Education and other state agencies as well were heavily influenced by the plantation's methods of control and supervision, and these agencies to this day rely on an obedient work force willing to bow to authority. The following organizational chart of Pioneer Mill is not unlike current organizational charts still used in these other agencies today.

109 "Case Study No. 5," 1
110 "Case Study No. 5," 3.

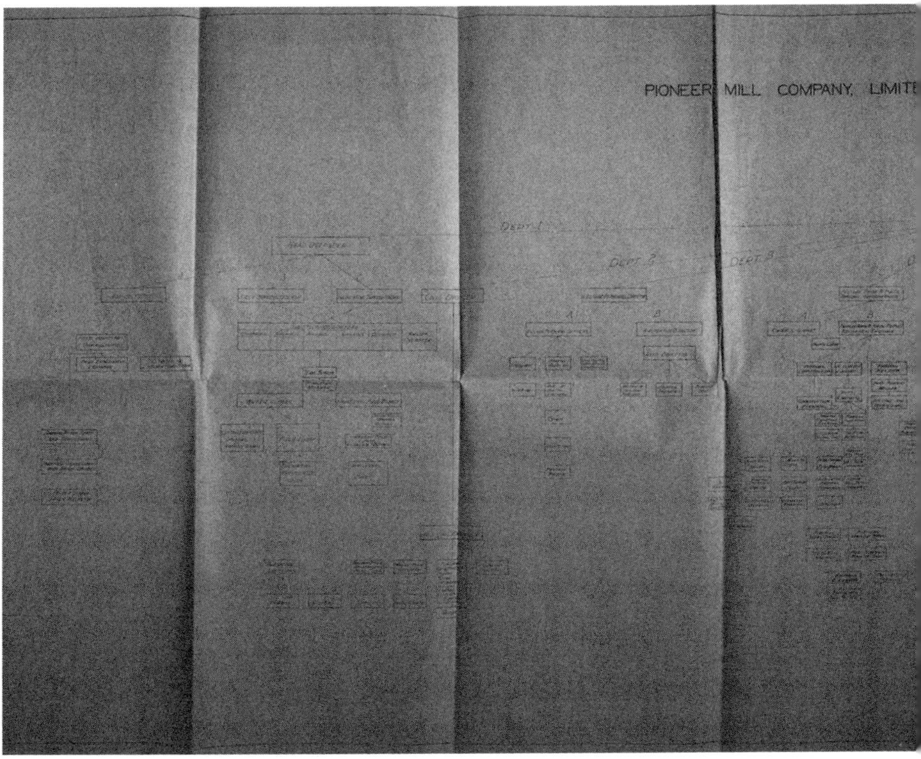

Pioneer Mill Company organizational chart. Courtesy of Bishop Museum.

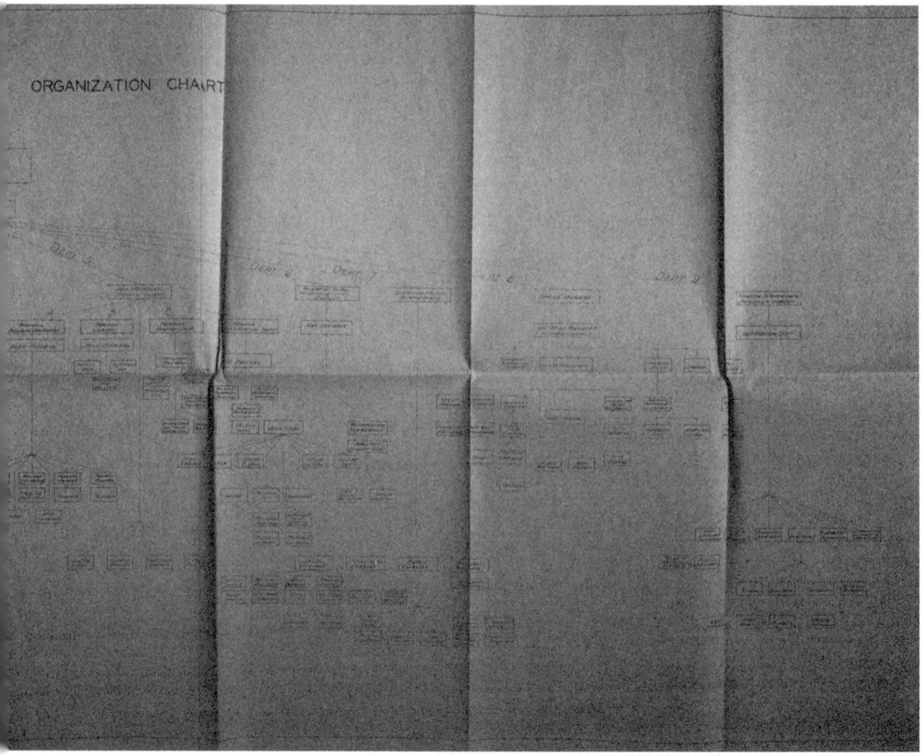
ORGANIZATION CHART
Dept 5
Dept 6
Dept 7
Dept 9

Despite, and maybe in some ways because of this structure, workers were later wary of the "Green Fields" initiative proposed by Pioneer Mill. And there is no doubt that many often told experiences of the laborers were positive.[111] These stories further illuminate life and livelihoods on the plantation. The Oral Histories Project for Pioneer Mill allows us a glimpse into the laborers' experiences:

> Pioneer Mill took care of all the employees. So we depended on the plantation... The plantation was really helpful. They used to do the house repair. And every summer they used to come grade the road. They really keep the camp clean. You know, pick up the rubbish. But plantation used to really take care the camp and the houses. We used to pay real minimal rent. Fifteen dollars a month. Water was one dollar a month. You raise your own vegetables and all that. Even if you have a big family, at least you can get by. [112]
>
> * * *
>
> My name is Fred Higuchi. I was born in Lahaina, the old Pioneer Mill Hospital, where it is now the Hard Rock Café. I spent

---

111 Amfac President Gary Grottke proposed the Green Fields principle in 1997, which would grant workers more freedom on the plantation. "Interestingly, I presented the idea as a benefit to workers, saying, 'You guys are going to love Green Fields, because now you're going to have the ability to make all these decisions.' Some people were actually freaked out by that. The union thought we were trying to stick them with the problem. We said, 'No. Amfac is still here; we're still in this thing together.'" Donne Dawson, "Amfac: New and Improved? The former Big Five company goes entrepreneurial," *Island Business*, August 1997, 17-22, p. 19.

112 James Higuchi, Oral History Interview, 252-253.

my young days in Pu'ukoli'i, a village of more than a thousand people. We had a public school, kindergarten to eighth grade. We had a Japanese (-language) school and we had a Methodist church, a Buddhist church, Catholic church, and that's about all as far as churches and schools.

Pu'ukoli'i Camp is located north side of Lahaina and we had all kind of people living there: Japanese, Filipinos, Chinese, Portuguese, Hawaiian, all nations, and we really got along together. We played ball, we went to school together, and best of all, after we graduate or leave the camp, when we see people outside we tell "Hey, howzit!"

You know, when we used to live in Pu'ukoli'i, we used (to) have families come to get together before New Year's and pound mochi. And everybody bring their share of the ingredients. After that we sit down and talk story, ate, made food. And eat the mochi and all. It was something that we all used to like 'cause they had a lot of food.

And they [Pu'ukoli'i] had a small little store, and we had barbershop. We had a theater that burned down. We used to have a public bathhouse, you know big bathhouse, one for the ladies, one for the men, and one for the Filipino families. The other groups, like the Haoles and the other people, you know, supervisors, they have their own bath [inside their homes]. But the regular people used to go down to the public bathhouse. It was good fun. [113]

* * *

113 Fred Higuchi, Oral History Interview, February 7, 2003 by Maria Orr, Biographical Summary, 276 & 278.

Oh, to us was a big occasion because we hardly got out from the camp. Every place we go we used to walk. From the camp, we used to go walk up the mountain. So we go walk pick guavas, oranges, bananas, all in the valley. All the places we go, we used to walk.

So when we played sports, we go to the other camps to participate. Plantation used to furnish all the transportation. Even when we formed our football team... We used to go on the weekends. Plantation used to supply us with the shoulder pad and head gear (chuckles) and then uniform. And then they supply the transportation. They sponsored the team. Then basketball, same thing. Yeah, we were really kept occupied. So to me, I never felt neglected or disgusted. So busy playing and going to school and all that. [114]

* * *

Like I told my men before we left the plantation, there's life after Pioneer Mill. Pioneer Mill was not the buildings. Pioneer Mill was the people, and as long as we're around, Pioneer Mill will be around, and the good times we had there will always be with us.[115]

The plantation helped some workers buy their own homes, and the deep friendships made on the plantation continued well into retirement. Also reverberating throughout the communities was the sense of building local culture—the

114 James Higuchi, Oral History Interview, February 5, 2003 by Maria Orr, 255.

115 Edward Hussey: Biographical Summary, Oral History Interview, 471.

subculture of local food, music, and pidgin language, etc. These are all aspects that began on the plantation, and they continue to inform the larger local community today.

But the growth of labor unions and strikes also occurred in this climate. By the mid 1930s and 1940s, after close to a century of prosperity, the sugar industry faced a bigger challenge than dry weather and water diversions—this one in the form of a disgruntled labor force. Worker strikes from this time period are recorded in the daily newspapers as workers began to unionize and demand more rights and better working conditions. On Maui, it was through water irrigation, and attempting to halt the free flow of water, that the laborers made their point. In December 1946, *The Honolulu Advertiser* reported that Pioneer Mill was under pressure from the union and laborers at Olowalu:

> The violence which flared at this plantation during the 79-day sugar strike was based entirely upon whether the cane fields should be irrigated.
>
> The ILWU-CIO stand was that the cane should die if their terms were not met, even if the plantations were permanently shut down and thousands of workers unemployed. [116]

The union directive at the time was that there was to be "'No water until the strike ends or we fight'": "Joseph Kaholokula, president of Local 144, ILWU, in a speech at a mass meeting

116 "Attack on 2 Vets, Mate Black Chapter on Maui," *The Honolulu Advertiser*, December 14, 1946, p.1, c.2.

on Oct. 18 ordered his men to stop the irrigation and fight if necessary."[117]

During these years, and during lengthy union talks and negotiations, Pioneer Mill faced massive stop-work days that turned into weeks. At various times more than 300 to 430 workers walked off their jobs at both of the Mill's sites in Pu'unene and Lahaina. In one long lasting stop-work period, workers from the Pu'ukoli'i camp caused Mill operations to come to a standstill:

> Approximately 430 Filipinos employed by the Pioneer Mill Co. at Lahaina, Maui went on strike early today when the management refused to accede to their demands to reinstate two Filipinos who were discharged on Wednesday.
>
> All of the men on strike, who are cane cutters, cane loaders and laborers on various other jobs, live at the plantations's camp at Puukolii. [118]

Another episode at Olowalu resulted in the violent attacks on three managers, and the "discharge of 11 union workers by the plantation management" followed.[119] During this time "The Pioneer Mill (was) completely shut down," and all workers except two men walked off the job.[120] *The Honolulu Advertiser* further reported that:

---

117 "Attack on 2 Vets, Mate Black Chapter on Maui," p.1., c.2.

118 "430 Filipinos Strike on Maui," *The Honolulu Star-Bulletin*, June 3, 1937, p. 21, c. 6.

119 "Pioneer Mill in Stalemate Over Firings," *The Honolulu Advertiser*, p. 3, c. 6.

120 "Nine Pioneer Mill Employes Let Out (sic)," *The Honolulu Star-Bulletin*, November 21, 1946, p. 1. C. 4.

> The alleged attacks were made in the Olowalu district on Nov. 6 on Pioneer officials Harlow Wright and on Michael Nelson and James B. Backlund. The men were supervisors of Pioneer and were on company property when groups of strikers were alleged to have beaten them for attempting to irrigate cane fields.[121]

This incident occurred during a strike, and served to lengthen the strike time. *The Honolulu Advertiser*, run by those sympathetic to the sugar planters, reported the dire conditions of the strike in mostly anti-union ways. One newspaper article was entitled "Pioneer Mill Workers in Virtual CIO Slavery,"[122] while another article reported:

> At Lahaina, Maui, where citizens and plantation workers are now shackled to a virtual terror reign that has supplanted law and order, a signed contract, and mutual understanding, the nerve-wracking strain of four months of unemployment is tragically apparent. 'Key union overlords' (who) declare themselves above the law and enforce their swaggering rule with gangster tactics.[123]

121 "Pioneer Mill Co. Workers' Attack Cases Continued," *The Honolulu Advertiser*, December 21, 1946, p. 4, c. 5.

122 "Pioneer Mill Workers In Virtual CIO Slavery," *The Honolulu Advertiser*, December 16, 1946, p. 1, c. 3.

123 "Strike Strategy of ILWU Planned In Detail On Maui," *The Honolulu Advertiser*, December 15, 1946, p. 1, c. 7.

Eventually, this 124-day strike was settled with an estimated loss to Pioneer Mill of "6,000 tons of sugar" that "cost over $700,000."[124]

In a turnaround from withholding privileges, beginning in 1950, Pioneer Mill began making house lots and new homes readily available to their employees: "'It is our purpose,' says Jack [plantation manager], 'to provide employes (sic) an opportunity for home ownership on fee simple land that will not jeopardize the production needs of the plantation.'"[125] First dibs on homes went to Pioneer Mill employees. This plan was enthusiastically embraced by the workers, and "about 200 employees have bought property in the first two tracts or have shown their desire to buy."[126] Here was a chance to show the viability and continuity of the company, while ensuring the loyalty of the workers. This was also a chance for the immigrant and local labor force to achieve the American dream of home ownership.

And it was the first large-scale attempt by the plantation to subdivide valuable sugar lands. The subdivision of lands in West Maui accelerated in the years to follow. North Beach, Keka'a, was subdivided, with projections of becoming the next Ka'anapali—Pioneer Mill's answer to a waning sugar economy, a dying

---

124 "Voting Today, Work Return Set Thursday," *The Honolulu Advertiser*, December 30, 1946, p. 1, c. 6, and, "Pioneer Mill Estimates Loss at $700,000," *The Honolulu Star-Bulletin*, January 1, 1947, p. 5, c. 8.

125 "Pioneer to Sell House Lots," *The Honolulu Advertiser*, April 5, 1950, p. 19, c. 2.

126 "Home Ownership Being Pushed by Pioneer Mill Co.," *The Honolulu Star-Bulletin*, May 2, 1950, p. 20, c. 4.

company, and a growing tourism industry. The North Beach subdivision had challenges from the start because of the lessons learned by the community from the sudden growth of Ka'anapali. A now informed and questioning populace wondered at the intelligence of massive resort building, set in place without any restrictions or consultations with the local community. The fight to preserve, yet still develop this stretch of West Maui, would take place for at least two decades.

Chapter 3: Making the Subdivision—Ka'anapali and North Beach

I am writing this letter while sitting on the sand at North Beach thinking about how much money and how many jobs Amfac seems to think we'll be willing to trade for it. I really have asked over a thousand children how they feel about having this beach developed and only one said it would be okay.

And so I'm wondering what price would be enough for me never again to sit in this place with the peace, tranquility and sense of balance that only nature can provide. How much would I settle for, to come back and always have hordes of people scurrying about with their activities and noise, never again to walk here in the moonlight without lights and sounds of nearby crowded accommodations.

And how would I feel about taking any of this money, or spending it, and what would I say to the children after it is gone? What do we tell them now, when we speak of the legends here and why both parents work two jobs each in the hotels? That's just the way it is, because these are minimum-wage jobs and the big bosses in Chicago really don't care about what happens here on Maui. Otherwise things would already be different and better here, wouldn't they? The children have told me, loud and clear, that there is no price they will take for this beach. Let's show them the respect they deserve and listen to them. [127]

The making of the Ka'anapali/North Beach subdivision occurred alongside the economic downslide of the once prominent Pioneer Mill company. The production of Ka'anapali—Hawai'i's first large scale resort development—diversified a waning company and propagated the development of North Beach, with hopes of the same results to follow. But the winds of change through this area of Maui sparked community protests set on preserving North Beach as a community resource. That Keka'a was developed at all still stings some residents. Others find solace in the fact that at the very least the development did not go unchecked and unrestrained.

In the 1970s and 1980s, Pioneer Mill downsized and "was classified a 'distressed plantation' by sugar industry analysts."[128] The history of this Amfac plantation spans a century and a half in Hawai'i as a Big-Five giant and as the first local company to earn $1 billion in revenue during its heyday.[129] Earlier troubles leading to a 1974 Federal Trade Commission charge that

127 Sherri Carden, "Commentary of North Beach," *Haleakalā Times*, July 16-August 5, 1997, 7.

128 George Cooper and Gavan Daws, *Land and Power in Hawai'i: The Democratic Years* (Honolulu: University of Hawai'i Press, 1990), 179.

129 Tim Ruel, "Dynsasty in decline: Amfac, the first Hawaii company to earn $1 billion in revenue, is a shadow of its former self," *The Honolulu Star-Bulletin*, September 2, 2001, 1.

Amfac and other C&H sugar suppliers were price fixing cost the company several million dollars, and exposed a chink in the "Sugar King" armor.[130] Fending off hostile takeovers, but then succumbing to a corporate raid in the 1980s, Amfac went through internal changes that undermined the strengths of this local company. JMB Realty Corp., a Chicago based real estate company, bought Amfac in 1988 for almost $1 billion. Over the next couple of decades, the company "has gone from the largest conglomerate in the state—with 8,500 workers in the islands—to a development company with a few hundred employees." [131]

In 1997, the company restructured to become more diversified. The division was spelled out:

> Six separate operating divisions: sugar farming, coffee farming, water, golf, land, and property development. The sugar, coffee, and water divisions were part of the old agriculture division, with water consisting of the company's control of the rights to 300 million gallons of water per day, which was primarily used to irrigate sugar cane. The golf division managed three golf courses in Kaanapali and Waikele. The land division was responsible for selling or leasing the company's nonstrategic landholdings. It seemed likely that Amfac Property Development Corp. was the most important division of the future Amfac/JMB and that some of the other divisions may be jettisoned. The company stated

130 "Amfac/JMB Hawaii L.L.C. History," www.fundinguniverse.com/company-histories/amfac-jmb-hawaii-l-l-c-history/, 2.

131 Tim Ruel, 2.

that it planned to focus its future development activities on its Maui land parcels. [132]

Bankruptcy followed in 2002. Amfac was renamed Kaanapali Land LLC, and "Today the company is a fractured remnant of its former self."[133] The next logical step for the company under these conditions was to look for profit in another industry, one that could make use of prime agricultural land and a ready-made labor force. Tourism therefore overtook the sugar industry economically, as Amfac created the Ka'anapali Resort—Hawai'i's first successful destination resort. Ka'anapali proved so profitable that "During the early 1980s Amfac top management was reportedly willing to run Pioneer Mill at a loss, if necessary, subsidized by the Kaanapali resort." [134]

In this atmosphere, sugar land and people were transformed into tourism land and people, as prime real estate and hotel workers became the next wave of industry and labor:

> In rural areas the big resorts were seen as a means for wives to have jobs as well as their husbands who worked for the plantations; as replacement employment when plantations reduced their workforces or went altogether out of business; and as a way for the children of local working people to rise in the world. [135]

---

132 "Amfac/JMB Hawaii L.L.C. History," 4.

133 Jacy L. Youn, "Cropped Down," *hawaiibusiness.com*, 1.

134 *Land and Power in Hawai'i*, 184.

135 *Land and Power in Hawai'i*, 186.

Tourism took the place of the sugar plantation, and local people easily filled the ranks as they began to labor on the new plantations.

The land deeds granted and/or leased a century or so before for Ka'anapali and North Beach solidified Pioneer Mill's control of this entire area. A portion of this land—the 95-acres at North Beach—was to become the much-contested space known as the North Beach subdivision.[136] Subdivision and community building were now notions that went hand in hand. Pioneer Mill controlled so much land in West Maui that any subdivision plans in the second half of the 20th century completely dictated the direction of industry and social growth for the overall community and the entire Island.

Numerous land grants make up North Beach. A large portion of this area was deeded from Land Commission Award 76, Royal Patent 7661, originally granted to William Shaw. On March 5, 1849, this Irishman received large farms on Maui through Land Commission Award 76. Early on, North Beach was known as Keka'a, and even earlier it was known as the farm Haenanui. The Land Commission Award for Shaw's properties on Maui recorded:

> This is a claim to four farms or pieces of land on the Island of Maui, and is based upon a written agreement, made between the claimant and Hoapili Wahine with the approbation of his

---

136 Some documents refer to the acreage as 95 acres, while others say 96 acres. I do not edit their calculations.

present Majesty and Kekauluohi, the late Premier, on the 17th day of December 1840, which agreement reads as follows:

> The Claimant's title is made clear by the above agreement and we do therefore, confirm and award to the Claimant William Shaw the lands "Haenanui," "Loinui" and "Waiolimu" on the Island of Maui, according to the annexed surveys of Theophilus Metcalf, Esquire, to have and to hold, to him, and his Hawaiian born heirs forever.[137]

Shaw's large tracts of land included property into the mountains and along the sea. For example, the Loinui farm alone contained all of the southern pali of Honokowai Valley, including all of the Honokowai River "from its source to its mouth."[138] William Shaw's landed estate on Maui was massive in the mid 1800s.

Patrick Shaw, William's son, sold a portion of LCA 76 after his father's death in 1879 to Henry (Harry) Turton:

> Know all men by these presents that we Patrick Shaw and Lahele Shaw wife of the said Patrick Shaw Island Maui Hawaiian Islands, for and in consideration of the sum of Two Thousand dollars to us in hand paid by Henry Turton of Lahaina Maui aforesaid the receipt whereof is hereby acknowledged do hereby give grant bargain sell and convey unto the said Henry Turton

137 Land Commission Award 76, Volume 1, page 225-230, Bureau of Conveyances, Honolulu, Hawai'i, 225.

138 Land Commission Award 76, 230.

> his heirs administrators and assigns forever—a certain tract or parcel of land situate in Honokowai Kaanapali Island Maui. [139]

Turton, a Canadian by birth and a citizen of the Hawaiian Kingdom, was a brick mason who later became the owner of multiple businesses and business ventures. He was also a cousin by marriage to Charlotte Iaukea, my great great grandmother. He created Pioneer Mill with James Campbell and eventually sold his interests back to Campbell and Paul Isenberg after declaring bankruptcy. James Campbell went on to become a dominating industrialist in Hawai'i, and built a powerful empire with the beginnings of what is today the Campbell Estate. Both Campbell and Turton had offspring with women of Hawaiian Ali'i rank, further ensuring their continuity in Hawai'i. The following excerpt briefly describes the business relationship between Campbell and Turton:

> Becoming interested in the cultivation of sugar cane, and having accumulated some capital by building and repairing houses and ships, Mr. Campbell started a plantation at Lahaina in 1861, and for a time was in competition with King Kamehameha V, who was endeavoring to promote a sugar estate in that vicinity. The King's lands later came into Campbell's possession. Hard work brought success, and in the early 70s, in partnership with the late Mr. Harry Turton, Mr. Campbell founded the Pioneer Mill at Lahaina, the forerunner of the present great plantation operated by the

139 Land Deed P. Shaw & wife To H. Turton, Book 62, Page 46-47, Bureau of Conveyances, Honolulu, Hawai'i, 46.

Pioneer Mill Co. Mr. Campbell realized the value of land and constantly increased his holdings; he once owned the land where the present town of Lahaina now stands, his possessions giving him the name under which he was known to the Hawaiians, "Kimo ona miliona" (James the Millionaire). Turton met with many business reverses; eventually the whole plantation came into Campbell's hands and he became sole owner until he sold it to H. Hackfield & Co. [140]

West Maui proved valuable for this sugar plantation because of the fresh water that could cultivate the entire district. Ka'anapali was also used for the loading and unloading of sugar and cattle just offshore. So, gaining control of the land and water was the primary imperative, and for those reasons land was leased or bought in large tracts that covered this entire area. The other Land Commission Awards and Royal Patents that make up the total area at North Beach are:

Being a portion of the premises described in Land Court Certificate of Title No. 658,559.

All of the lands described in and covered by Royal Patent 4818, Land Commission Award 6601, Apana 4 to Piimoku;

Land Patent Grant 13332 to Pioneer Mill Company, Limited;

140 Edited by George F. Nellist, "The Story of Hawaii and Its Builders," *The Honolulu Star-Bulletin*, Hawaii, 1925.

Royal Patent 6653, Land Commission Award 5121 Apana 1 to Kane;

And being also portions of the following:

Royal Patent 4594, Land Commission Award 4241 Apana 3 to Kaluakini;

Royal Patent 7661, Land Commission Award 76 Apana 2 to

William Shaw;

Royal Patent 1684, Land Commission Award 5005 Apana 2 to Keoni (John White);

Royal Patent 3939, Land Commission Award 6722-B Apana 1 to Mai;

Royal Patent 7995, Land Commission Award 3689 Apana 2 to Maui;

Royal Patent 3559, Land Commission Award 5002 Apana 4 to Kahanaumaikai;

Parcel A, Land Patent Grant S-15081 to Pioneer Mill Company, Limited;

Parcel C, Land Patent Grant S-15081 to Pioneer Mill, Limited;

Royal Patent 6297, Land Commission Award 6601 to Piimoku; and

Royal Patent 3023, Land Commission Award 3987 Apana 1 to Holona.

Situate at Honokowai, Kaanapali, Lahaina, Maui, Hawaii [141]

This land entirety is represented in the following maps. They further illustrate the ahupua'a and land titles for the area.

141 Helber, Hastert and Kimura, Planners, *North Beach, Kaanapali, Maui, Final Environmental Impact Statement*. Planning Department, County of Maui, Hawai'i, October 1987, Exhibit D, Legal Description of Lots 1-4 of Ka'anapali North Beach.

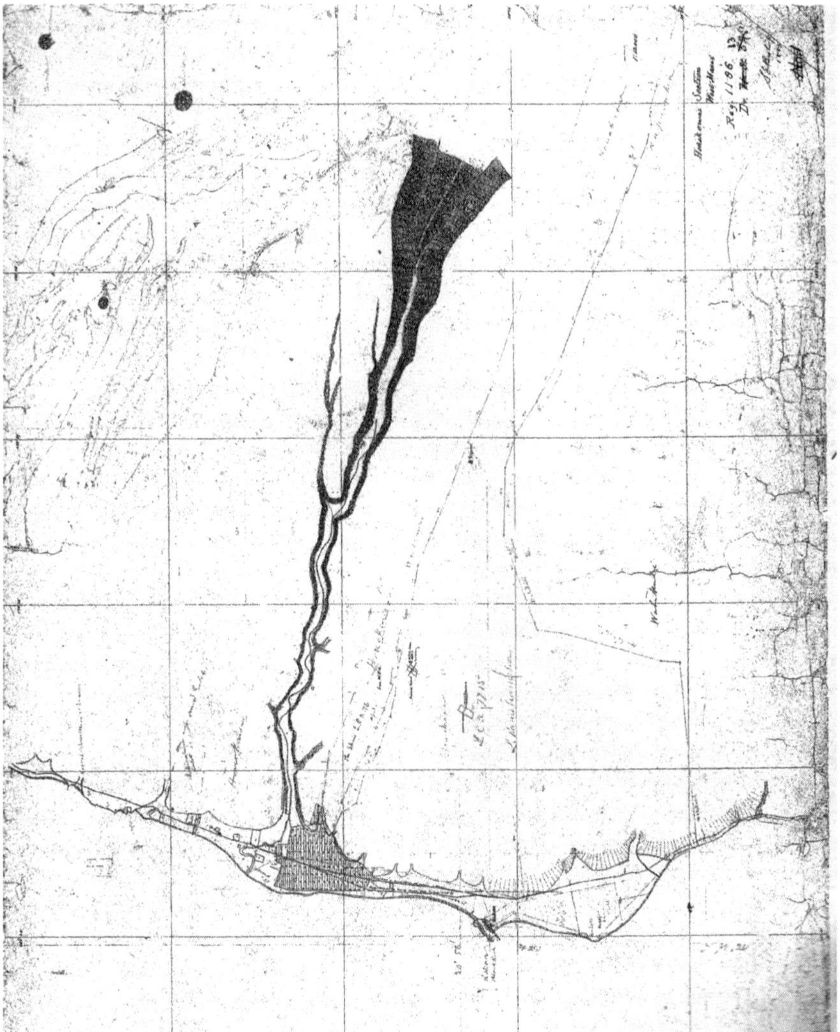

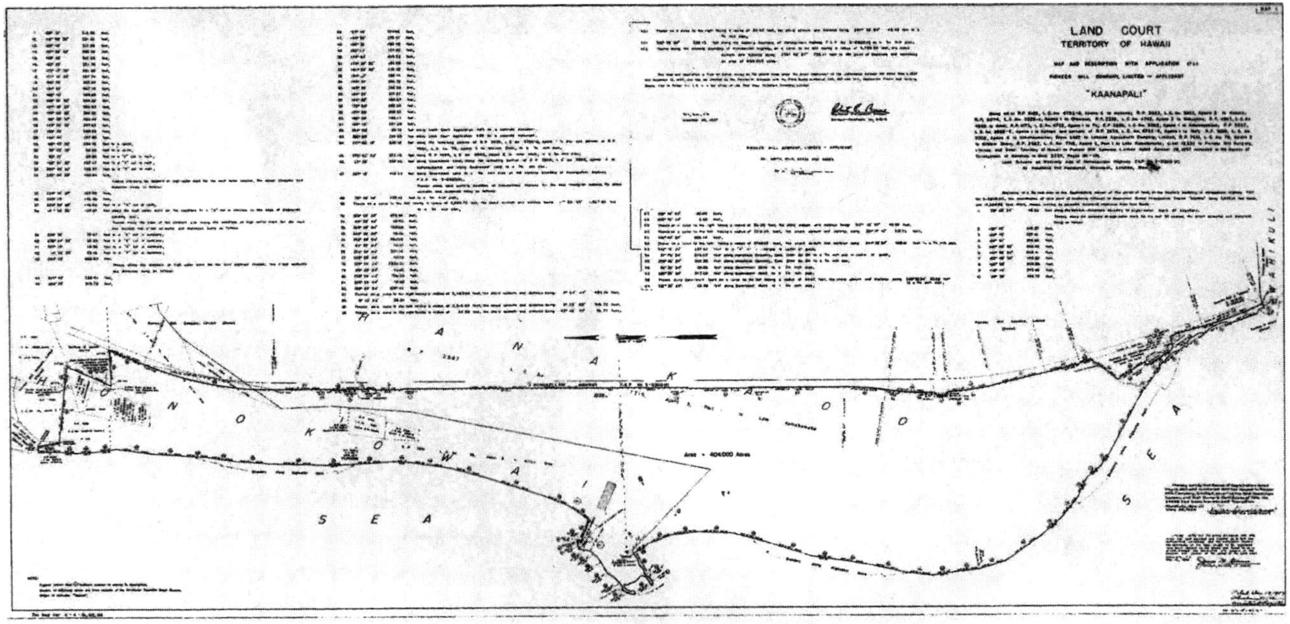
LAND COURT
TERRITORY OF HAWAII
"KAANAPALI"
SEA
SEA

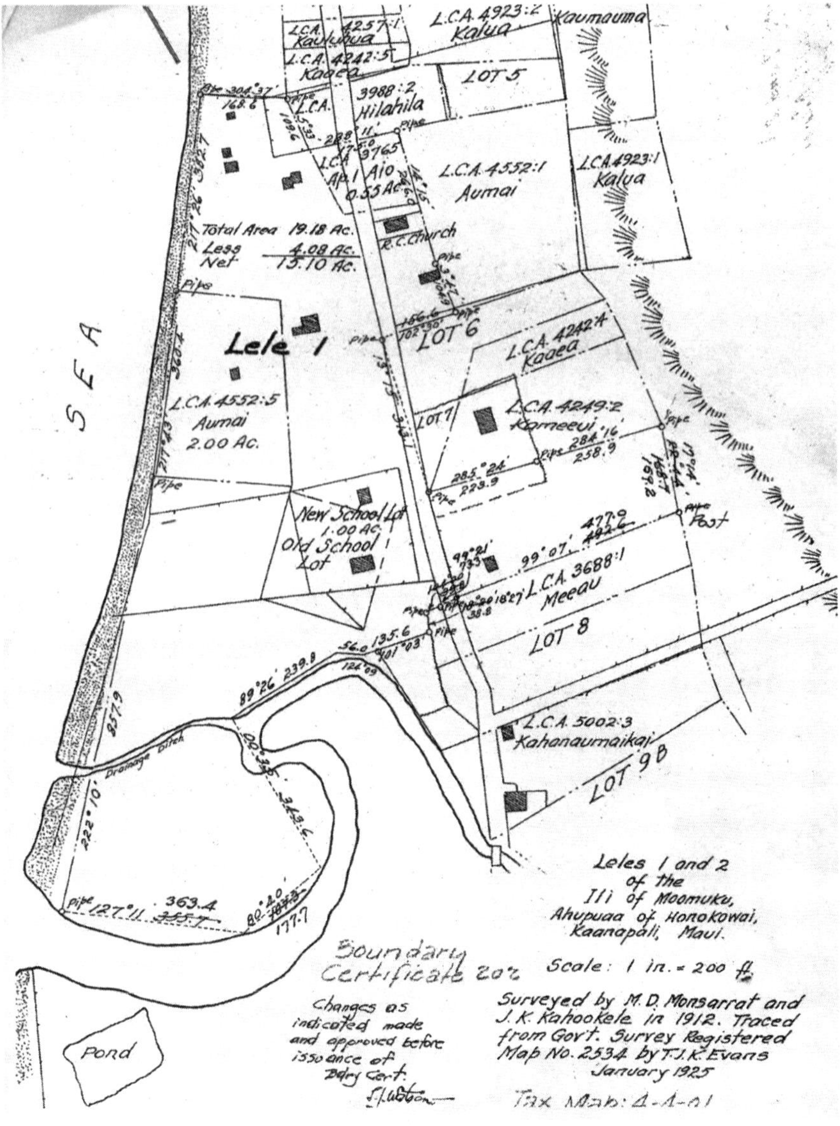

L.C.A. 4257:1
Kaukuwa
L.C.A. 4242:5
Kaaea
L.C.A. 4923:2
Kalua
Kaumauma
LOT 5
L.C.A. 3988:2
Hilahila
L.C.A. 3765
Ap. 1 Aio
0.55 Ac.
L.C.A. 4552:1
Aumai
L.C.A. 4923:1
Kalua
Total Area 19.18 Ac.
Less 4.08 Ac.
Net 15.10 Ac.
R.C. Church
LOT 6
SEA
Lele 1
L.C.A. 4552:5
Aumai
2.00 Ac.
L.C.A. 4242:4
Kaaea
LOT 7
L.C.A. 4249:2
Kameeui
New School Lot
1.00 Ac.
Old School
Lot
Post
L.C.A. 3688:1
Meeau
LOT 8
L.C.A. 5002:3
Kahanaumaikai
LOT 9B
Drainage Ditch
Pond
Leles 1 and 2
of the
Ili of Moomuku,
Ahupuaa of Honokowai,
Kaanapali, Maui.
Scale: 1 in. = 200 ft.
Boundary Certificate 207
Changes as indicated made and approved before issuance of Bdry Cert.
Surveyed by M.D. Monsarrat and J.K. Kahookele in 1912. Traced from Gov't. Survey Registered Map No. 2534 by T.J.K. Evans January 1925
Tax Map: 4-4-01

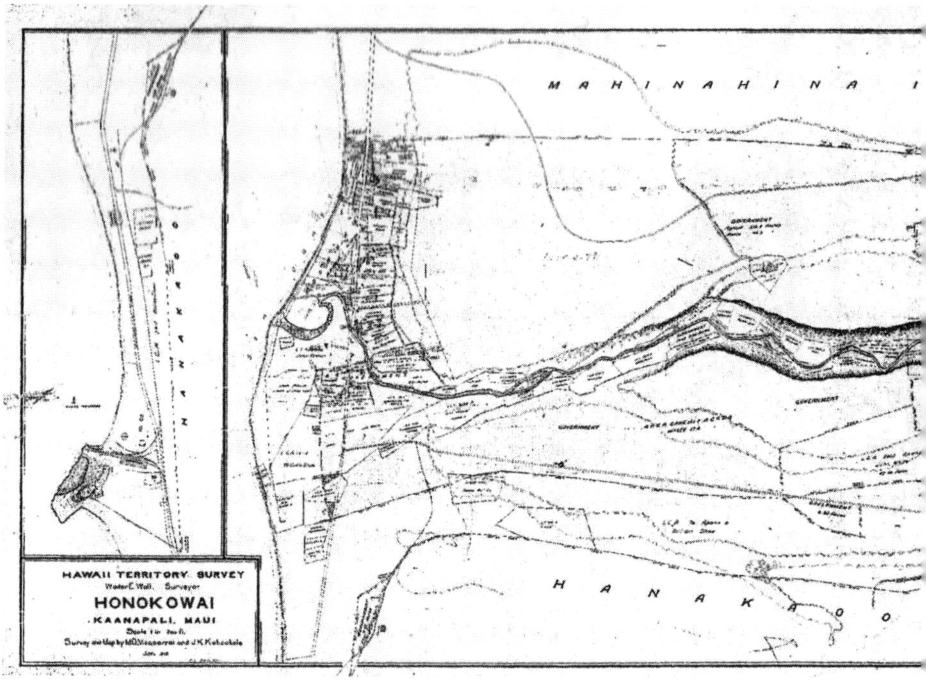
MAHINAHINA
HANAKAOO
GOVERNMENT
HAWAII TERRITORY SURVEY
Walter E. Wall, Surveyor
HONOKOWAI
KAANAPALI, MAUI

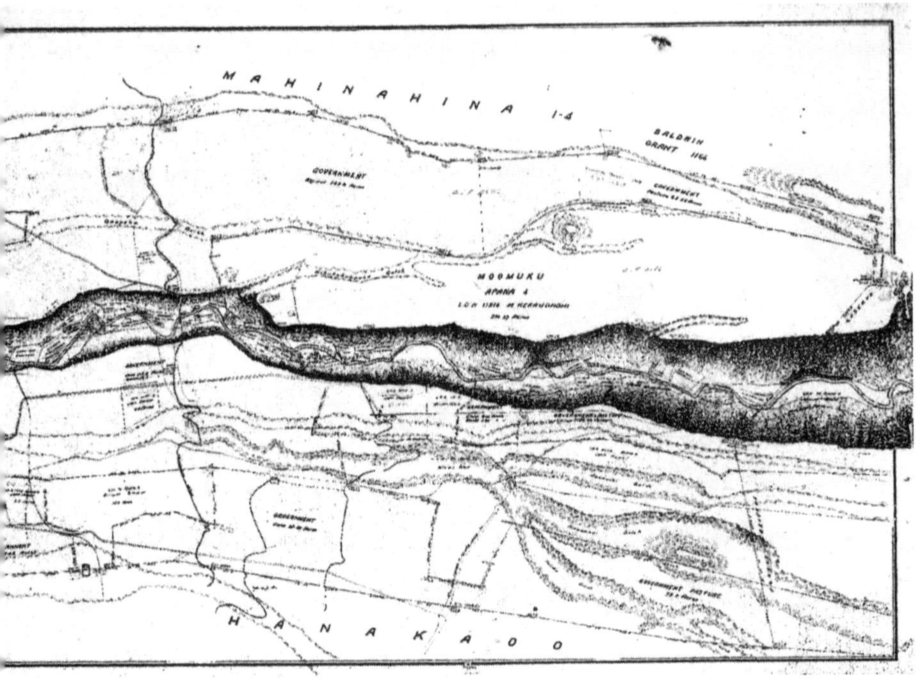
MAHINAHINA 1-4
BALDWIN GRANT 1166
GOVERNMENT
GOVERNMENT
MOOMUKU
APANA 4
GOVERNMENT
GOVERNMENT PASTURE
HANAKAOO

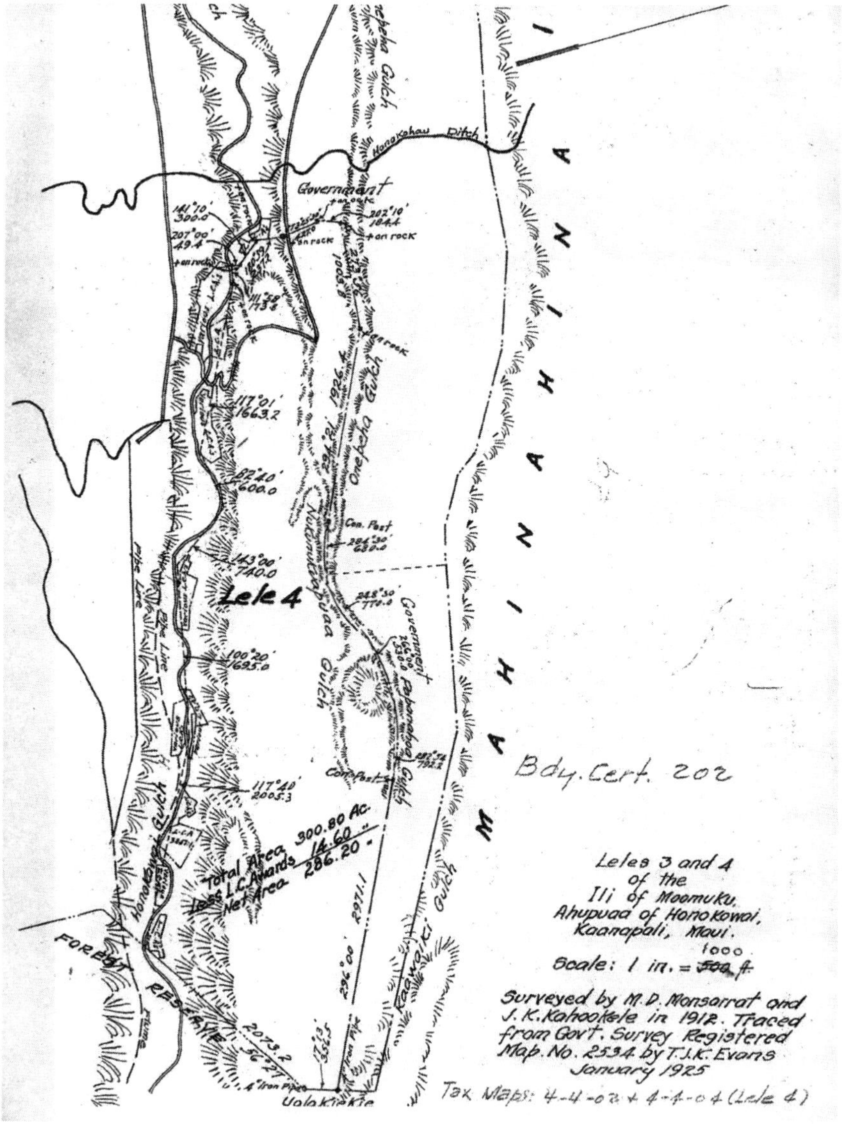
Lele 4
Government
Honokohau Ditch
Onepeha Gulch
Honokowai Gulch
Kaawaiki Gulch
Pipe Line
Con. Post
FOREST RESERVE
Uolakiekie
MAHINAHINA
Total Area 300.80 Ac.
Less L.C. Awards 14.60 "
Net Area 286.20 "
Bdy. Cert. 202
Leles 3 and 4
of the
Ili of Moomuku,
Ahupuaa of Honokowai,
Kaanapali, Maui.
Scale: 1 in. = 1000 ft.
Surveyed by M.D. Monsarrat and
J.K. Kahookele in 1912. Traced
from Govt. Survey Registered
Map. No. 2534 by T.J.K. Evans
January 1925
Tax Maps: 4-4-02 + 4-4-04 (Lele 4)

North Beach, Ka'anapali, was part of the subdivision order granted on May 26, 1960 by the applicant Pioneer Mill Company, Ltd., and filed as Application No. 1744, for Original Certificate of Title No. 80,096.[142] The Final North Beach Environmental Impact Statement in 1987 contains the following narrative of land ownership:

> The proposed project site of approximately 95 acres is located on the leeward coast of West Maui, Lahaina Judicial District. The proposed site is on the tax map key 2nd Division, 4-4-01: por. 02, 03, 06, 08, 09, and 68, and 4-4-02:24 and 4-4-06:5. The Amfac Property Investment Corporation and Tobishima Pacific, Inc. own the property in fee. This area is the last remaining beachfront hotel area of the Kaanapali Master Plan.
>
> The unimproved 95-acre ocean-front property was formerly the site of the Kaanapali Airport, and still contains the remnants of the abandoned runway, vacant terminal area and parking lot. Sugar cane fields cover approximately three-fourths of the project area. Also present are limited areas of kiawe forest, strand vegetation, and koa-haole scrub. All airport structures have been removed, and the old runway has been broken up. The parcel runs north-south along the shoreline, on the makai side of the Honoapiilani Highway. The site is gently sloping from north to south and from the highway to the beachline, with an average slope of one percent. Access to the site is provided by Kai Ala Drive, the old airport driveway off the Honoapiilani Highway.
>
> The southern boundary of the proposed site is adjacent to

142 Land Court Applications, Applicant Pioneer Mill Company, Ltd., Original Certificate of Title No. 80,096, Application No. 1744, Bureau of Conveyances, Honolulu, Hawai'i.

> the established Kaanapali Beach Resort, specifically the Maui Kaanapali Villas condominiums and the Royal Lahaina Hotel. The northern boundary of the site abuts the 12-story Mahana condominium in the resort area of Honokowai. The property contains approximately 3,400 feet of ocean frontage to the west. The eastern edge of the site (mauka portion) abuts the Honoapiilani Highway. Uses directly mauka of the highway include sugarcane fields, a cluster of rental car outlets and the Lahaina Wastewater Treatment Plant.
>
> The subject property is identified as Land Commission Award 76, Royal Patent 7661, Apana 2 to William Shaw issued in 1849. Upon Shaw's death, the land was conveyed by his heirs to Henry Turton, Paul Isenberg and Walter Horner and Lahaina Agricultural Company and conveyed to Pioneer Mill Company in 1884. All previous uses of the site were for growing sugarcane and as a cattle pasture. [143]

After subdivision plans were entered and Ka'anapali developed, the plans for resort and condominium development of North Beach were put forth in 1987. The owner was now registered as Amfac Property Investment Corporation and Tobishima Pacific, Inc, and the project was called the Ka'anapali North Beach Joint Venture. In the 1990s during the effort to downsize sugar cane production because of Amfac's dwindling economic prominence, and declared bankruptcy in 1999, the idea of a resort destination—which had proven successful with

143 Helber, Hastert and Kimura, Planners, *North Beach, Kaanapali, Maui, Final Environmental Impact Statement*, II-1 & II-4.

Ka'anapali—once again took center stage. The growth of North Beach along similar lines is explained in the following Final Environmental Impact Statement from 1987:

> In the early 1950s, Amfac conducted land use evaluations and feasibility studies on the use of the Kaanapali property as a visitor destination resort. A Master Plan for Kaanapali was developed, encompassing 1,200 acres, including the subject site incorporated hotel, commercial, recreational and residential uses. In 1959, development of the Kaanapali Beach Resort directly south of and adjacent to the subject site was begun with the construction of a water system, sewage treatment plant, drainage system and a network of roadways. Today, nearly 30 years later, approximately half of the original 1,200-acre master plan area has been developed.
>
> The current Kaanapali Master Plan calls for hotel uses on the site (makai of the Honoapiilani Highway, north of the Puukolii Road intersection). The surrounding undeveloped areas mauka of Honoapiilani are planned for a mix of commercial, golf course, resort condominium and residential uses. The state-proposed mauka by-pass highway would run east of and roughly parallel to Honoapiilani Highway. The proposed development is consistent with Amfac's original plan for the Kaanapali area.[144]

To be developed, North Beach would have to be re-classified for non-agricultural usage:

144 Helber, Hastert and Kimura, Planners, *North Beach Kaanapali Final Environmental Impact Statement*, II-4.

> The subject property is presently utilized for sugarcane production, although it is designated as Urban district by the State Land Use Commission, zoned for hotel use by Maui County and designated for hotel, park and open space by the Lahaina Community Plan. [145]

Also noted in the EIS was the specific socio-economic class that still mostly resides in Ka'anapali:

> Unlike Lahaina, Kaanapali has very few year-round residents. Of the 579 permanent residents in 1990, many were retired, and the rest were almost exclusively managers, executives, and professionals working in the hotels and related businesses of Kaanapali. They were 85% Caucasian, and more than half had moved into their homes within the last five years. These residents and their families mostly live in the upscale homes of the South Beach Mauka area, built on the hillsides and surrounded by golf courses.
>
> The population of Kaanapali also includes visitors, short-term residents, and resort workers. On a given day an estimated 9,000 people stay in Kaanapali—a number equal to the whole population of Lahaina. Another 5,500 direct employees commute into Kaanapali from Lahaina or further away. [146]

Because a mostly white and wealthy population resides in

---

145 Helber, Hastert and Kimura, Planners, *North Beach Kaanapali Draft Environmental Impact Statement*, Planning Department, County of Maui, Hawai'i, August, 1987, IV-3.

146 PBR Hawaii, Prepared for AMFAC Properties, *Final Environmental Impact Report, Puukolii Village, Volume II*, January 1993, 2.5-2.6.

this area, a commuter population emerged on Maui. Residents have to travel across the island to and from work daily, while managers and tourists live and vacation near Ka'anapali.

By 1993, Ka'anapali had become an important economic center for Maui, which further encouraged the tourism growth model for the entire northern area of West Maui:

> In the 1950s, AMFAC withdrew about 500 acres of West Maui land from kiawe, sugar, and grazing to create the Kaanapali Resort, Hawaii's first master-planned resort. The master plan covers a total of 2,000 acres and currently includes two 18-hole golf courses, six major hotels with almost 4,000 rooms, over 1,300 condominium units, and several hundred single-family custom homes. After Kaanapali proved successful, the Kapalua resort (developed by Maui Land and Pineapple) began development. Visitor units, mostly condominiums, have also been built at Honokowai, Kahana, and Napili in West Maui.

The success of Ka'anapali as a visitor destination is strongly emphasized in all of the development documents, and the connections between Ka'anapali and North Beach were repeated often:

> The adjacent Kaanapali Beach Resort is considered by many to be the world's first master-planned destination resort. Originally conceived over thirty years ago, it has transformed an arid, scrub brush land into a successful world-class destination resort. Kaanapali Beach Resort is the single largest employer on Maui, and in 1985, had gross revenues of about $35 million for its 5,000 employees. The Kaanapali Beach Resort currently

experiences the highest occupancy and the highest achieved room rates of the major multi-purpose resorts in the State.

The proposed North Beach resort is likewise expected to have significant positive socio-economic impacts through job creation, visitor expenditures, and increased public (tax) revenues. An economic and fiscal impact study (John Child & Company, December 1986) projects [positive] economic and fiscal impacts on the local (public and private sectors) as a result of the project. [147]

This positive projection assessed the land as empty and available—ready to be developed into another world-class destination resort, and therefore easily transcribable into the tourist gaze. The "tourist gaze," is the title of John Urry's book, and describes tourism's complex social structure.[148] Urry discusses how both nature and native are neutralized, and then systematically reimagined, within the constructs of the tourist economy. In other words, land/native first have to be made visible and visitable in order to be gazed upon. And this endeavor takes some manipulation of the natural. The visitor economy provides the frame whereby places/people are first imagined and then visited—as the entire point is to come, see, have the experience, and leave. Within this agenda, superficial understandings are formed and reinforced.

This model also assumes the local people will be easily

---

147 Helber, Hastert and Kimura, Planners, *North Beach Kaanapali Final Environmental Impact Statement*, V-35 & V-37.

148 John Urry, *The Tourist Gaze* (Thousand Oaks, California: Sage Publications, 1990).

incorporated as workers in this tourist economy. Any unforeseen and foreseen costs to the people/environment are the by-products of the industry and therefore permissible and even justified. That tourism economies actually create poverty and near poverty conditions in their environments is never directly addressed. Ingeniously, tourism creates a large outflow of capital to multi-national corporations, strains the public sector that subsidizes this all-encompassing industry, and broadcasts a practiced misrepresentation of place based on a pre-packaged "reality." All these aspects are written into the tourist gaze.

In 1987, North Beach seemed to fit this gaze seamlessly:

> Analyses of various on-site environmental features have found the North Beach property to be well endowed with physical attributes that are desirable both as amenities in a resort development and for their own sake. These attributes include the ocean-front location, marine recreational opportunities, pristine near-shore waters, and dry, warm climate. The studies have also indicated that the proposed development is compatible with the existing natural environment... Improved public access to the shoreline will result from the project, enhancing the recreational resources of the West Maui community. The project will result in the conversion of land used for sugarcane production to non-agricultural activity... Direct, full-time employment opportunities and temporary construction employment will be generated by the project, and these in turn will have benefits that ripple through the regional economy. Public revenues from excise, personal and property taxes are expected to more than offset any expenses associated with the expansion of public services

to meet the requirements of the development and indirect population growth. [149]

The original plans for the 95-acre North Beach site varied. One plan was to subdivide the land into eleven lots for up to six hotels and two public parks planned for the south and north ends. There was also speculation that development would consist of just one large hotel. The only other option was to leave the land fallow. The multi-hotel initiative endured, with various reasons offered—first and foremost, the need for hotels to satisfy Maui's tourism industry: "Overall, the market study indicated very clearly that there will be a continued large, unmet demand for higher priced accommodations, which North Beach could fill." [150]

The other reasons for development included employment, because of the expected increase in construction jobs; the idea that the land was already designated for hotel use in the Lahaina Community Plan, the Maui County General Plan, and the Hawai'i State Plan, which all called for the growth of the visitor industry; the claim North Beach development would be "complimentary to resident lifestyles (as) park and beach access (would) be provided;" and finally

---

149 Helber, Hastert and Kimura, Planners, *North Beach Kaanapali Final Environmental Impact Statement*, "Relationship Between Local Short-Term Uses of the Environment and Maintenance and Enhancement of Long-Term Productivity," Chapter VIII.

150 Helber, Hastert and Kimura, Planners, *North Beach Kaanapali Draft Environmental Impact Statement*, III-7.

> The increase in visitor industry jobs is particularly important in light of Amfac's recent decision to reduce its Lahaina Pioneer Mill Sugar Company operations. The reductions are necessitated by the presently high production costs, low sugar prices, and the lack of sufficient amounts of high quality, low cost water for irrigation. [151]

Resort development at North Beach seemed to add up to nothing but benefits for tourists, locals, the environment, the County of Maui, and the State of Hawai'i. The overall development plan for the area specified that "Hotel construction is expected to occur during subsequent phases extending up to a ten year period. Existing zoning designations would allow up to 4,900 hotel units, but a maximum of 3,200 units is anticipated."[152] So apparently infallible in its logic, this version would seem to make it impossible to weed out any negatives for this project and others like it. Despite the glowing forecasts given by the planners for the North Beach development in the 1987 Environmental Impact Statement, however, a growing list of concerns was being readied by the larger community, which will be discussed in the next chapter.

---

151 Helber, Hastert and Kimura, Planners, *North Beach Kaanapali Draft Environmental Impact Statement*, III4-III-7.

152 Helber, Hastert and Kimura, Planners, *North Beach Kaanapali Final Environmental Impact Statement*, I-2.

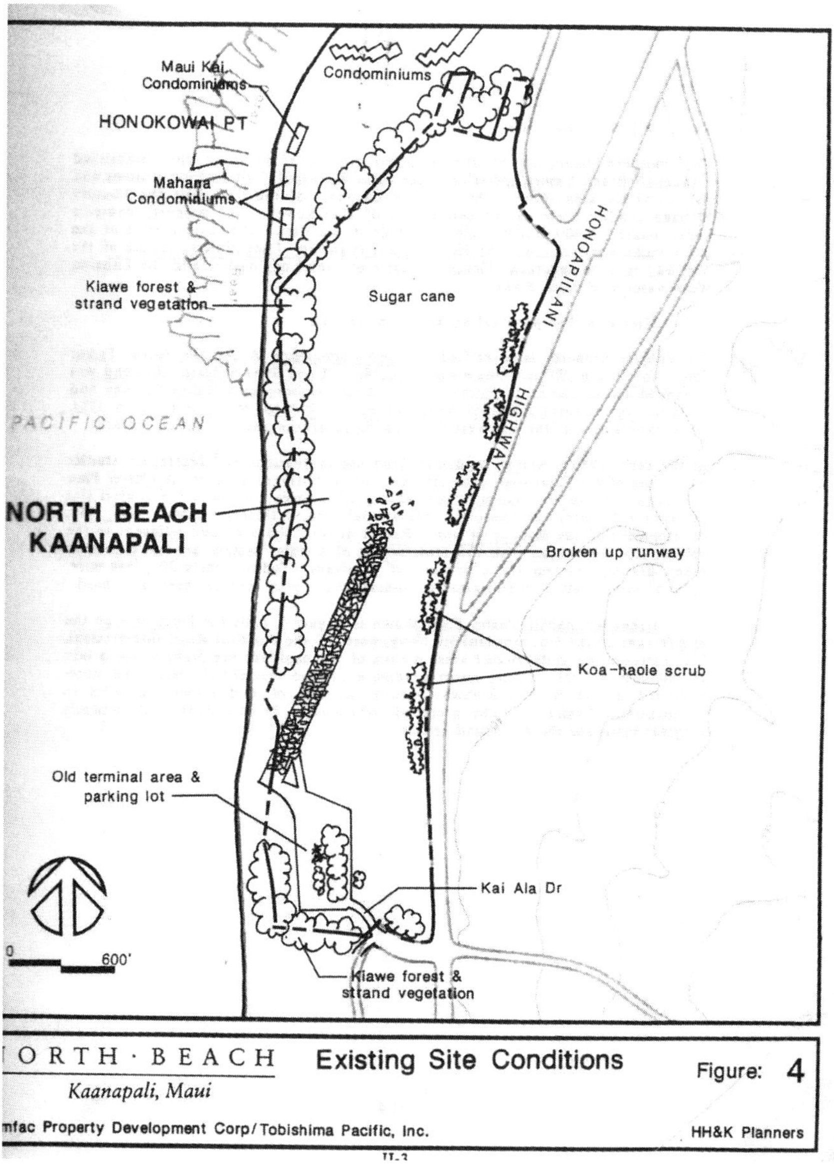

Helber, Hastert and Kimura, Planners, North Beach Kaanapali Final Environmental Impact Statement, II-3.

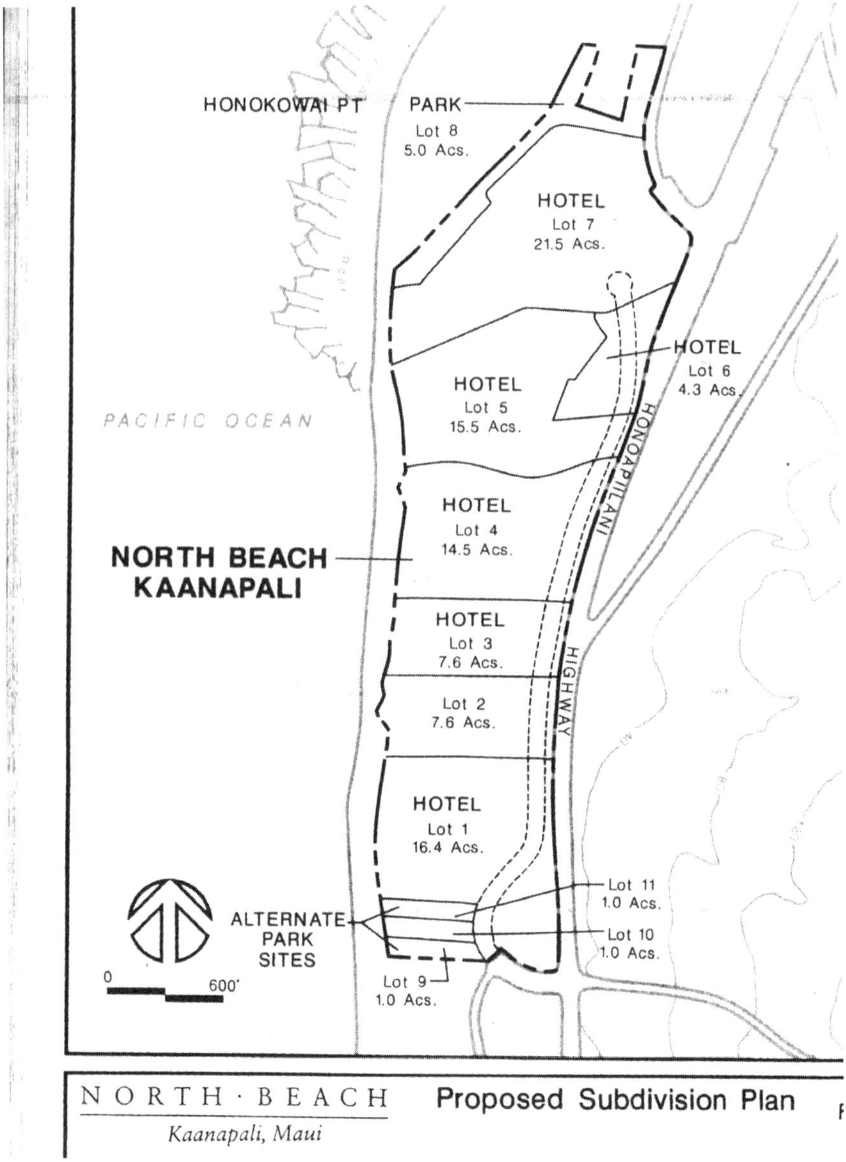

Helber, Hastert and Kimura, Planners, North Beach Kaanapali Final Environmental Impact Statement, III-2.

With the plans to develop North Beach came the realization that low-income housing for workers would have to be provided. In the 1980s, a section of the land leased to Pioneer Mill in Wahikuli was to become the Villages of Leali'i project for affordable housing. The ground breaking was scheduled for 1990, but the project lagged, and Environment Hawai'i reported that "The state Board of Land and Natural Resources has bowed to Pioneer Mill, a tenant of the state that has acted more like its master." [153]

On February 24, 1994, the lease of 1,800 acres of state land in Wahikuli by Pioneer Mill expired. The state then paid Pioneer Mill an unprecedented $750,000 on February 25, 1994 for the costs of moving the cane roads and parts of the irrigation system, even though the company had received many allowances during its decades long leases:[154]

> General Lease S-4229 allowed Pioneer Mill the use of 1,820 acres of state-owned land on the slopes of West Maui above Lahaina. For most of the 25-year duration of that lease, however, Pioneer Mill's rental payments were based on cultivation of far less land than that. [155]

And with regards to the water:

---

153 "HFDC Must Pay Amfac $750,000 to Leave Unencumbered State Land, Bond Says." *Environment Hawai'i*, Aug. 1, 1994 v. 5 n. 2, 1.

154 *Environment Hawai'i*, 1.

155 *Environment Hawai'i*, 7.

General Lease 4329 [was] sold at public auction to Amfac. Amfac agreed to pay $9 per million gallons (1.50 per million gallons of pumped water) for water taken between 1956 and 1966. For 1966 to 1970, Amfac would pay $10 per million gallons for the first 360 million gallons it took annually and $8 per million gallons thereafter. For the four years of water withdrawals from Kahana Valley, Amfac agreed to pay the state a lump sum of $160,588.32.

By comparison, the rate charged homeowners on O'ahu is $1,650 per million gallons ($1.65 per thousand gallons). [156]

Multiple issues surround the Villages of Leali'i. Besides these allowances granted to Pioneer Mill by the government, the Villages of Leiali'i was also the site of a decades long battle regarding the State's presumed "right" to sell 1,033 acres of ceded lands to meet West Maui's housing shortage. Leali'i, located next to the Lahaina Civic Center, faced court challenges for over a decade, until Act 176 stated the state's "right" to sell ceded lands with a two-thirds vote from each house of the State Legislature. The court case that decided this records the history:

The instant action arises from the [State's] efforts in the mid-1990s to transfer certain parcels of ceded lands to private entrepreneurs for the purpose of residential development. On August 11, 1995, the plaintiffs [(including Osorio)] filed suit, seeking an injunction against the [State] from selling or otherwise transferring to third parties two specific parcels of ceded lands

156 *Environment Hawai'i*, 12.

> located on the islands of Maui and Hawai'i as well as any ceded lands from the public lands trust. Alternatively, the plaintiffs [(including Osorio)] sought a declaration that the State was not authorized to alienate ceded lands from the public trust or, if the trial court ruled the State was so authorized, a declaration that. . . . such alienation would not limit the claims of native Hawaiians to the ceded lands.
>
> On December 5, 2002, the trial court ruled in favor of the [State], concluding that the plaintiffs' [including Osorio's] claims were barred by the doctrines of; (1) sovereign immunity; (2) waiver and estoppel; and (3) justicability—specifically, political question, ripeness, and the mandate against advisory opinions. Nevertheless, the trial court also concluded that the State had the express authority to alienate ceded lands from the public lands trust. [A Hawai'i Rules of Civil Procedure (HRCO)] Rule 54(b) [(2007)] judgment was, thereafter, entered on January 31, 2003, and the plaintiffs [(including Osorio)] appealed. [157]

This landmark case listed the plaintiffs as the Office of Hawaiian Affairs (OHA) and individuals, including Professor Jonathan Osorio, versus the state and then Governor Linda Lingle, for attempts at disposing ceded lands to private developers. Linda Lingle, the former Mayor of Maui County, was already well versed in the plantation's initiatives with this parcel of land. The Plaintiffs sited the Apology Resolution, signed by U.S. President

157 *Office of Hawaiian Affairs v. Housing and Community Development Corporation of Hawaii (HCDCH)*, In the Supreme Court of the State of Hawai'i, No. 25570, Appeal From the First Circuit Court, October 27, 2009, 2-3.

Clinton on November 23, 1993 as Public Law No. 103-150, 107 Stat. 1510 (1993), as giving rise to "fiduciary duty on the part of the State—as trustee of the ceded lands—to preserve the corpus of the public lands trust until 'such time as the unrelinquished claims of native Hawaiians have been resolved.'"[158] The U.S. Supreme Court sent the case back to the State Supreme Court and noted that the jurisdiction does not fall under the Apology Bill to be used as leverage because ceded lands is a State matter.

OHA and the other plaintiffs, except for Osorio, withdrew the case in 2009 after Act 176 became law. This law stated that any proposed sale of ceded lands would go before the Legislature as a Concurrent Resolution:

> Act 176 requires legislative approval prior to the alienation of any lands from the public lands trust, including (1) ceded lands, i.e., lands that were 'classed as government or crown lands previous to August 15, 1895,' or (2) lands to which the Hawai'i housing finance and development corporation holds title, which in this case is the Leialii parcel. [159]

And in reaction to Osorio's appeal:

> Based on the foregoing, we hold that (1) Osorio has standing in this case, but (2) his asserted claims are not ripe for adjudication because there has been no final action by the legislature (or any

158 *Office of Hawaiian Affairs v. Housing and Community Development Corporation of Hawaii (HCDCH) & Id.* At 197-210, 217, 177 P.3d at 907-21, 927, 3.

159 *Office of Hawaiian Affairs v. Housing and Community Development Corporation of Hawaii (HCDCH)*, 13.

agency) under Act 176 with regard to the Leialii parcel or any other ceded lands. [160]

This deal struck between the State and OHA put the sell of ceded lands to a two-thirds Legislative vote. Osorio has not abandoned the case. Should the attempt to sell ceded lands arise anew, besides legislative approval, the racial argument already sparked of determining who qualifies as Hawaiian, and has the right to bring forth the case, may become a primary contention—and not the fact that ceded lands are in actuality seized lands by the United States and therefore not legally at option to be sold. As it stands currently, Leiali'i is not built, outside of the development of roughly 60 acres that initiated the court case, and so the contested acreage of roughly 1,098 is now 1,033 acres. This remaining acreage is currently undergoing all the preliminaries to being developed. But as stated in The Villages of Leiali'i EIS:

> On July 13, 2009, the Governor signed into law Act 176, Session Laws of Hawai'i 2009 which requires a community meeting, appraisal, and two-thirds vote approval of each house of the Legislature to convey State land in fee simple to third parties.
>
> Given the ceded lands issue, HHFDC intends to lease property or comply with Act 176 at the Villages of Leiali'i. [161]

---

160 *Office of Hawaiian Affairs v. Housing and Community Development Corporation of Hawaii (HCDCH)*, 13.

161 Belt Collins Hawaii Ltd., *Environmental Impact Statement, The Villages of Leiali'i Affordable Housing Project, Lahaina, Maui*, Hawai'i, March 2010, 6-7.

In 2012, Governor Abercrombie accepted the Final Environmental Impact Statement for the Villages of Leali'i.[162] Construction is expected to begin in 2016. The proposed development is noted in the West Maui Community Plan Update:

> Villages of Leiali'i—This project is planned by the State Housing Finance Development Corporation and situated mauka of Honoapiilani Highway in the vicinity of the Lahaina Civic Center and Wahikuli Terrace comprising an area of approximately 1,120 acres. The planned residential community will include approximately 4,813 housing units to be developed in phases, an 18-hole golf course, two elementary school sites, neighborhood business commercial uses, church, child care, recreational/park uses, and other public uses. [163]

Pu'ukoli'i Village is the other affordable housing initiative by Pioneer Mill that has not been built to date. The now re-named Pu'ukoli'i Village Mauka was finally approved to proceed in 2009 after many years of debate and debacle. Pu'ukoli'i Village is slated for development on 260 acres of Amfac lands once partially occupied by the sugar plantation camp of the same name. In 1994 it was written up as follows:

> Pu'ukoli'i Village—This project is proposed by AMFAC/JMB, a Hawaii Corporation, in the vicinity of the former Puuolii Village

---

162 Neil Abercrombie *Re: Acceptance of the Final Environmental Impact Statement for the Villages of Leiali'i Affordable Housing Project*. December 7, 2012.

163 *Community Plan Update, Proposed West Maui Community Plan*, Maui Planning Department, September, 1993, 16.

> and comprises an area of approximately 299 acres. The proposed residential community is to include approximately 1,700 housing units to be developed in phases as well as sites for neighborhood commercial uses, hospital/emergency medical facilities, child care center, church, elderly housing, elementary school, and a community park.[164]

Linking the development nostalgically to the original Pu'ukoli'i Village, the plan claimed that:

> During the heyday of West Maui's sugar industry, in the first half of this century, plantation camps for the workers of Pioneer Mill and Maui Land and Pineapple Company dotted the area. Puukoliii was the largest of these. It was a self-contained town with separate Japanese and Filipino camps, a theater, a ball park, Japanese baths, a church, a school, shops, and at times as many as 2,000 residents. Many of Lahaina's older residents have fond memories of Puukolii Village. Milton Murayama's award-winning book All I Asking For Is My Body depicts plantation camp life in old Puukolii, under the fictionalized name 'Pepelau.' The plantation camps grew smaller and finally disappeared as employment in the West Maui sugar industry dwindled to a few hundred. [165]

This passage links labor to housing, and sugar to tourism, without missing a beat. The romanticized images of the housing

164 *Community Plan Update, Proposed West Maui Community Plan,* 16.

165 PBR Hawaii, *Final Environmental Impact Report Puukolii Village, Volume II,* January 1993, 2-1—2-2.

might also cause one to ignore the fact that native uses for the land are ignored here. The narrative ties the past Pu'ukoli'i to the present Pu'ukoli'i without too much interruption or anticipation of the narrative.

In contrast, the first Environmental Impact Report readied specifically for the Pu'ukoli'i development painted a more realistic account of contemporary life in West Maui. The report, by PBR Hawai'i for Amfac Properties Investment Corporation, was blunt about the negative impacts that unrestrained development was already having on West Maui. There was a dire need for affordable housing for the population of hotel workers who commute to work. The report linked the nostalgia to the current realities—the newer plantation, in the form of hotels, needed to provide living space for the new plantation workers—busboys, wait-help, and maids:

> Hotel employment alone accounts for one-third of the jobs in West Maui. It is estimated that more than half of Maui's economy depends directly or indirectly on the visitor industry. [166]
>
> Lahaina and the rest of West Maui have experienced a severe housing shortage since the 1970s.[167] Indications of crowding, shared quarters, and high housing costs in West Maui are visible in the results of the 1988 DBED Tourism Impact Core Survey.[168]
>
> Part of the psychological 'growth strain' people are feeling

166 PBR Hawaii, *Final Environmental Impact Report Puukolii Village, Volume II*, 2-6.

167 PBR Hawaii, *Final Environmental Impact Report Puukolii Village, Volume II*, 2-5.

168 PBR Hawaii, *Final Environmental Impact Report Puukolii Village, Volume II*, 2-12.

> in West Maui comes from seeing rapid growth and development, particularly in the visitor industry, while not having enough housing and community facilities to meet residents' needs. The community facilities at Puukolii Village should help ease that sense (of) strain by balancing the needs of residents with those of the visitor industry. These facilities may also add to West Maui's sense of self-sufficiency in terms of having jobs, housing, (and) community facilities all located within West Maui. [169]
>
> Two decades of rapid growth in West Maui have put strains on the area's infrastructure and affordable housing supply. The concerns of West Maui residents strongly center around these two issues. Lack of affordable housing is a dominant concern for most residents, especially renters, with the cost of living, traffic, and infrastructure issues following close behind. These immediate concerns, along with approaches to long-term growth management, occupy much of the agenda of the current Community Plan update process. [170]

Although this is an accurate account of the housing situation and other issues in West Maui, the main purpose of this particular document was still to fast track the affordable housing development, which many in the community opposed because it introduced yet more development without an overall realistic study of the impact of that development on West Maui residents.

In 1996, Pu'ukoli'i was passed without an EIS, which was

169 PBR Hawaii, *Final Environmental Impact Report Puukolii Village, Volume II*, 5-6.

170 PBR Hawaii, *Final Environmental Impact Report Puukolii Village, Volume II*, 2-2.

"waived for this project since there were 'no adverse findings on the original EIS (done in 1992-93) to the West Maui Community.'"[171] The community was upset. In a letter to (former long-time) Maui County council member Wayne Nishiki, Jo Anne Johnson Winer (current Director of Transportation for Maui and former intervenor in the North Beach Lot 1 development), wrote:

> We disagree with the original EIS findings and feel that a great deal of the data is flawed. The project bypassed the County and was processed under Act 15 by the State. The original project presented to the State has been altered, and we feel that these major changes will adversely affect West Maui residents. [172]

George Montgomery agreed:

> It is, I believe, inappropriate to 'waive' an environmental impact study (even if the law could be so tortured in construction) when it is painfully obvious that there is inadequate water, sewer and drainage as well as roads for ingress and egress. [173]

Linda Crockett Lingle, Maui Mayor in 1996, responded to Jo Ann Johnson Winer by letter:

> As you know, this project was approved under the State

---

171 Letter from Jo Anne Johnson Winer to Wayne Nishiki, Maui County Council, October 2, 1996.

172 Letter from Jo Anne Johnson Winer to Wayne Nishiki.

173 Letter from George C. Montgomery to Mr. Blanco Re: Puukolii Village AMFAC.

> Act 15 provisions which allow a developer of an affordable housing project (by State definitions) to bypass the usual County permitting process. The County therefore has very limited authority over the specific activities being proposed as part of this development. [174]

Pu'ukoli'i Village was supposed to be for affordable housing, but Amfac was required to build affordable housing anyway. That this area is now surrounded by multi-million dollar homes prompted Amfac to plan market-value homes alongside the area periphery and closest to the neighbors:

> Besides traffic, there may be concerns about the appropriateness, or social 'fit' between affordable housing and these custom, single-family homes. Project planning responds to such concerns, in that market housing will be located along the project boundary. The project homes nearest to existing upscale residences will be fairly large, with landscaped sections. [175]

Pu'ukoli'i Village is still not built, and many of the upscale homes along the periphery have been foreclosed, as the land market has not been as profitable as hoped by the developers.

Because of these cases, community involvement ramped up in the 1990s and early 2000s in West Maui. This united desire to grow the area responsibly was the impetus behind what is

---

174 Letter from Linda Crockett Lingle to Jo Anne Johnson Winer Subject: Proposed Puukoliii Village Development, September 16, 1996.

175 PBR Hawaii, *Final Environmental Impact Report Puukolii Village, Volume II*, 5-7.

currently known as Ka'anapali 2020, Amfac's final project in Hawai'i for almost 5,000 acres in West Maui.[176] In this case, Amfac is asking for community involvement in the planning of this area. How seriously Amfac will listen to those voices is still yet to be determined, but the multiple issues arising from the development of Ka'anapali, North Beach, and other areas have highlighted the need for community participation in the planning.

Community planning for Ka'anapali 2020 began when "10 community members agreed in early 1999 to define the parameters for a community-based planning process for 4,325 acres in the Kaanapali/Honokowai area owned by the applicant's affiliates."[177] Specific to the Ka'anapali area, the plan did not reach into Kapalua or Lahaina. The area covered first included the 96 acres at North Beach, 917 acres at Lower Honokowai, 1,050 acres at Middle Honokowai, 775 acres at Honokowai Mauka, 1,187 acres of the West Maui Forest Reserve, and 300 acres from the Honokowai Gulch.[178] Within this area, "Pioneer Mill Company uses approximately 1,000 acres of their agricultural lands in Kaanapali to grow seed corn."[179] The seed is sold to Monsanto.

The group invited eight community stakeholder groups,

---

176 Tim Ruel, 7.

177 Munekiyo and Hiraga, Inc., *Kaanapali 2020 Plan, Environmental Impact Statement Preparation Notice*, February 2005, 1.

178 Munekiyo and Hiraga, Inc., *Kaanapali 2020 Plan*, 3.

179 Munekiyo and Hiraga, Inc., *Kaanapali 2020 Plan*, 37.

with eight representatives from each group—including Amfac, Cultural Heritage, Community Organizations, Government, and others—to take part in the *Kaanapali 2020: Making It Pono* conference, held from November 4-6, 1999.[180] This group focused on agriculture, education, and water resources. Its findings were presented to the Land Plan and Economic Feasibility Group in February 2000.[181] At the "reunion" meeting later that year, the group set forth the following vision statement:

> **Vision for Kaanapali 2020**
> Kaanapali 2020 Will Have Places
> What kind of places?
> Places to work, public places, places to play, places to learn, quiet places, private places,
> Places to till the soil, places to preserve our heritage, places to exercise,
> Places to shop, places to relax, fun places, places to gather our families,
> Places to grow things, places to live, places to walk or bike,
> Places to get well, places to protect our resources,
> Places to raise our families, places to remember
> Green places, places to visit
> Places to be proud of! [182]

It was also then decided that the number of places should

180 Munekiyo and Hiraga, Inc., *Kaanapali 2020 Plan*, 1.

181 Munekiyo and Hiraga, Inc., *Kaanapali 2020 Plan*, 3.

182 Munekiyo and Hiraga, Inc., *Kaanapali 2020 Plan*, 3.

be reduced. The second reunion conference on August 14, 2002 excluded:

> The 96-acre North Beach, the 1,187-acre West Maui Forest Reserve area, the 300-acre Honokowai Gulch, the 808-acre agricultural areas in Middle Honokowai and the approximately 775-acre Honokowai Mauka since land entitlements are not required.[183]

What was in the Plan was 914 acres in Lower Honokowai and 240 acres of Puukolii Village in Middle Honokowai—hardly a cohesive vision for Ka'anapali.[184] As noted in the 2005 Environmental Impact Statement for Ka'anapali 2020, things had changed dramatically:

> The original plan covering approximately 4,325 acres was presented at the first Kaanapali 2020 "Making It Pono" Reunion in 2000. Continued committee input and refinement brought about amendments to the original concept. Plan adjustments resulted in excluding North Beach makai lands, the conservation lands, Honokowai Mauka lands, agricultural lands in Middle Honokowai and portions of Honokowai Gulch from the Project Area since land entitlements were not required for these areas. Further refinements to the original plan involved relocating the Puukolii Village concept to the Lower South Honokowai area, with priority given to the establishment of affordable and employee housing early in the development phase. Other major

183 Munekiyo and Hiraga, Inc., *Kaanapali 2020 Plan*, 5.

184 Munekiyo and Hiraga, Inc., *Kaanapali 2020 Plan*, 5.

> changes involved reducing the golf course development from two (2) to one (1); and lowering the overall units proposed from 3,515 to 2,810. [185]

Further:

> Kaanapali Development Corporation (the 'Applicant') proposed to implement a land use plan, known as 'Kaanapali 2020 Project Development Area Plan', for approximately 1,154 acres at Kaanapali, Maui, Hawaii, owned by its affiliates, Pioneer Mill Company Limited, Amfac Property Investment Corp., Amfac Property Development Corp. and Amfac/JMB Hawaii, LLC.
>
> The Kaanapali 2020 Project Development Area Plan reflects the vision of the West Maui community for the future uses of the approximately 1,154 acres. This vision includes a mix of residential, recreational, open space, golf course, public/quasi-public and commercial uses. [186]

Whether this plan actually "reflects the vision of the West Maui community" is debateable; some members are opposed to the plans set forth in Ka'anapali 2020. Reasons are various, but the most basic one is that the land slated for development requires zoning changes from agricultural to residential and urban:

> Therefore, to implement fully the Kaanapali 2020 Project Development Area Plan, the following requirements are

185 Munekiyo and Hiraga, Inc., *Kaanapali 2020 Plan*, 78.

186 Munekiyo and Hiraga, Inc., *Kaanapali 2020 Plan*, 5.

> required: (a) a State Land Use District Boundary Amendment to Urban District for those lands in Lower Honokowai now designated as Agricultural district; (b) a West Maui Community Plan Amendment from Agricultural, Open Space and Project District 3 to a new Project District 3 designation encompassing the approximate 914-acre Lower Honokowai area and the approximate 240-acre Puukolii Village area east (mauka) of the proposed Lahaina Bypass; and (c) a County Change in Zoning for Lower Honokowai and the approximate 240 acre Puukolii Village area mauka of the proposed Lahaina Bypass from the Agricultural and R-3, Residential zoning district to Project District 3, coupled with the adoption of a site specific Project District zoning ordinance containing specific performance standards.[187]

On these rezoned lands will sit parks, single and multi-family residences, a proposed trolley system, and dedicated pedestrian, gold cart, and bicycle lanes. The "Smart Growth" principle espoused by the project focuses on mixed living ideals, and is estimated to take approximately fifteen years to build.[188] The output has yet to be realized.

North Beach in many ways sparked this sense of community consciousness. The grass roots initiatives reimagined what residents could and should expect from developers in their own backyard. In this atmosphere, environmental and cultural understandings and community recognition were becoming widespread threads in developmental priorities across the state.

---

187 Munekiyo and Hiraga, Inc., *Kaanapali 2020 Plan*, 7.

188 Munekiyo and Hiraga, Inc., *Kaanapali 2020 Plan*, 15-24.

Massive land and water use by the big plantations was now being publically questioned and challenged. Culture and ʻāina should be considered in land planning, and so should the realities of the low-income, low-paying workforce created by sugar, and continued by tourism. These ideas and agendas began to gain traction and even became realized during this time period on Maui.

Even so, the challenge remained, and continues today, to change the mindset that once permitted unquestioned allowances to big business in Hawaiʻi, and especially on Maui. Getting off the plantation is easier to imagine than accomplish, because it takes a paradigm shift regarding the purpose of land and people and industry. For many years, local history and livelihoods have reflected the economic rhetoric of two industries—sugar and tourism—and tourism still has a stranglehold on government and individual perceptions of growth and opportunity. Despite a growing awareness of environmental and cultural preservation, those growing up on Maui still come to believe that the economic possibilities are limited. Seeing beyond this horizon, or just beyond the visible and invisible power structures, takes imagination and hope.

Chapter 4: "It's Keka'a, Not North Beach!" The Battle Over Lot 1

Resort development in Hawai'i has its critics. Hotels and condominiums often impact local communities negatively, and these effects are usually not fully appreciated until long after the public testimonies pointing out the obvious have been completed, the planning permits for projects up against critical public commentary are approved, and the encroachment of developers into communities that once knew other ways of life besides the tourist economies has taken place. The material and psychological effects on local communities are harder to pinpoint once the "tourist gaze" and its supporting structures have lodged themselves. We grow accustomed to a service-oriented economy and outlook. We become accustomed to the physical and emotional poverty that this entails.

Some of the results associated with resort development are poor infrastructure planning, rising land costs that attract outside investors and therefore preempt locals from buying property, the marginalization and destruction of native habitats and people, and the presentation of such development as natural, and supposedly caring for the land and people on which it encroaches. But economic profit does not care about caring. On Maui, sugar and hotels dominate the socio-economic strata and the panoramic landscape—naturalizing their presence by their very existence.

By the 1990s the developers of North Beach had a tougher road to travel, due to a now practiced local skepticism and scrutiny. *It's Keka'a, not North Beach* was a mantra that reassociated people with the ʻāina, leading to a rise in cultural awareness. Kekaʻa is one of the original names for the area, so using it sparked the fight to recognize the ʻāina itself. But even after years of community protest, Kekaʻa was still developed, though in a scaled-back version of the original plan due to community outcry, as many voiced their discontent at Maui County Planning hearings. One example of this activism was displayed by Lori Kaufman's third grade class at Princess Nahiʻenaʻena public school. Ms. Kaufman submitted a letter to the county planners and encouraged her students to speak out against the looming development.

Dear Maui County Planning Commission,

It has recently come to my attention that an area known as North Beach in Kaʻanapali, may soon be zoned for Hotels and Condos. This would be, in my opinion, a disastrous mistake.

I am a third grade teacher at Princess Nahiʻenaʻena Elementary School. When I told my 26 eight year olds that someone wanted to build Hotels and Condos along this stretch of untouched beach they gasped! When I told them there would be 3,200 rooms, they were astonished!

My students and I feel there are enough Hotels and Condos in the Kaʻanapali area. We would like to see some of the beaches left natural and undeveloped.

I moved to Maui 5 years ago. In that five years there has been too much building. Where once there was an open field, now houses have grown. Where once there were tall trees, now towering hotels stand. If this trend continues the children will not know what the natural beaches looked like.

The tourists who come to Maui don't come to see hotels and condos. Most of them come here to escape from the bustle of their lives. They want a place that's away from it all. If we put condos and hotels on every beach, soon the people of Maui will have to go elsewhere to escape.

Please stop the development of North Beach!
Say yes to Beaches!
Say no to Buildings!

Sincerely,
Lori Kaufman
Third Grade Teacher
Princess Nahiʻenaʻena
Lahaina

Kaufman's students submitted the following signs and testimonies to the Maui Planning Commission's hearings, intended to discourage the impending zoning changes. Despite these pleas, the area zoning was changed from agricultural to commercial.

Dear Maui County Planning Commission

We don't want you to build some condose and hotels because we want to see the beauty of Ka'anapalis North Beach we want to feel the nature of Ka'anapalis North Beach. (sic)

Your Friend,
Kaliona Vierr
Princess Nahi ena ena

****

Dear Maui County Planning Commission

We would like you to not build hotels and other things around the North beach because if you build hotels around it then there will be no more beautiful beaches anymore and we want beautiful beaches. So if you are the ones that decide where the hotels are going to be then when they build it there will not be anymore beautiful beaches for yourself too. Now see how we feel and you feel too. So now don't build anything around beaches unless it's bathrooms or anything. (sic)

From,
Robin Lamarca
Princess Nahi'ena'ena Elementary school.

Dear Maui County Planning Commission,

I want to save North beach because that is my favorite beach. People can go swimming, fishing, snorkal and diving and the kids can play in the sand and have fun. People can lay down under the coconut trees and rest.

Sincerely,
Rochells Bucaneg
Princess Nahiʻenaʻena
Elementary School

****

Dear Sir,

If you don't want trouble please don't build hotels at North beach, Because we need open space. We don't care for money we care for beaches. We want a place to have fun. I want a beach to play in. We have enough hotels here, we need more space. If you build a hotel we will be very sad. You don't want to see sad people in your hotel or outside, don't you.

Sincerely,
Rojane Malijana
P.S. Please listen to us.

Besides the pleas from children, anti-development messages from the community poured in, leading eventually to direct involvement from community members in the overall planning process. What was more recently developed as Kaʻanapali 2020 is only the latest effort at community dialogue that began several decades ago.

It was the 1982 Lahaina Community Plan, updated in 1993 and renamed and reconceptualized as the West Maui Community Plan, that first included community voices in the overall development process. The updated version warned of the dangers of "unconstrained growth," and urged coordination of community resources for "future growth with [the] development of adequate infrastructure."[189] The Maui County 1990 General Plan Update also called for limits to the visitor industry and population growth "so as to preserve important community values."[190] The West Maui Community Plan proposed a complete guide for responsible growth for the entire region. The goal for land use was:

> An attractive, well-planned community with a mixture of compatible land uses in appropriate areas to accommodate the future needs of residents and visitors in a manner that provides for the stable social and economic well-being of residents and the preservation and enhancement of the region's open space areas and natural environmental resources.[191]

West Maui residents began to meet in 1991 to formulate this new Community Plan. Many of these residents also spearheaded the Citizens' Advisory Committee of the Lahaina Open Space

189 *Community Plan Update, Proposed West Maui Community Plan*, 9 &22.

190 PBR Hawaii, *Final Environmental Impact Report Puukolii Village, Volume II*, 3-1—3-2.

191 *Community Plan Update, Proposed West Maui Community Plan*, 13.

Society. A few were also named as the first intervenors in the North Beach Lot 1 development case. The following newsletter represents the pointed agendas put forth early on by the Lahaina Open Space Society.

Preserving our open space and culturally significant areas in the Lahaina Region

LAHAINA OPEN SPACE SOCIETY

ISSUE THREE - AUGUST 1997

Keka'a

Na Kupuna O Maui has respectfully requested that the area many of us refer to as North Beach (Old Airport Beach) return to its Hawaiian name, ***Keka'a*** In a letter addressed to the editor of the Maui News, Patty Nishiyama most eloquently teaches us about the significance of the site.

"As a representative of Na Kupuna O Maui and a Native Hawaiian who has resided on Maui's west side all of my life, I would like to respond to the July 20 editorial regarding North Beach.

The editorial states erroneously, and with assumed authority, that the area has no special significance culturally, historically or naturally. The ancient village of Keka'a, which is currently referred to as North Beach, was once the capital of Maui, under King Kaka'alaneo, and home to at least 3,000 Hawaiians. The village stretched from Makaiwi Beach where the Hyatt Regency Maui now stands to the Honokowai Stream. Within the boundaries were the sacred sites of Pu'u Keka'a, a heiau and burial mounds. The royal taro patch of Lo'i Hi'e, the royal fishpond of Loko I'a and Ke Ala Loa, the old King's Road, were also contained in the area.

Kupuna and I have personally located three sacred pohaku that clearly mark the boundaries of Keka'a. One of the pohaku has been desecrated and choked by the roots of a tree planted to hide it. Located on the Royal Ka'anapali Golf Course is a cave named Ke Ana Pueo where the guardian spirits are believed to dwell as owls. One of the best known spirits to have lived there was Wahine Pe'e, the hiding woman.

Pu'u Keka'a, which has been desecrated for many years, is of great spiritual significance as a sacred point where souls of the dead leaped into their ancestral spirit land. It was believed that only an individual of great spiritual strength could intrude into that world and escape without harm. Kahekili, the last chief of Maui, for whom Amfac named the park, leaped from Pu'u Keka'a. He was unharmed because of his great spiritual strength. Even visitors to Maui are familiar with the sacred and cultural significance of Pu'u Keka'a, also known as Black Rock.

The battle of West Maui between two brothers, Kamehamehanui and Kauhi, sons of King Kekaulike, took place in the area. Maui chants describe many aspects of Keka'a.

These are just a few of many facts that verify the spiritual, cultural and historical significance of the area. Much of this information can be found in Amfac's History of Kaanapali, 1981.

Perhaps whoever wrote the editorial failed to do the proper homework before verbally desecrating Keka'a (North Beach). Perhaps it would have been in order to exercise humility and consideration for the Native Hawaiians who are threatened with the loss of yet another area containing their history, spirituality, way of life, and the bones of their ancestors. Shame on you for being so insensitive and uninformed when addressing such an important issue."

Monday meetings

It's difficult to keep up with what's happening. Each week a new development unfolds just as we think we know whas up!

The task of saving Keka'a for the community is, to say the very least, multifaceted requiring constant vigilance, determined dedication, creativity and a large sense of humor.

The Lahaina Open Space Society meets on Monday nights at 5:30 in Lahaina at the Malu'ulu o lele Cultural Center across from the Wakida tennis courts.

We welcome new members and encourage new ideas. Besides it's an interesting way to spend your evening. Instead of watching the plot unfold on television, you can help us write the script.

Please join us. Call Patty Nishiyama at 667-6936, Louise Rockett at 669-6311 or JoAnne Johnson at 661-3237.

◆◆◆◆◆◆◆◆◆

Non-profit application status

The Lahaina Open Space Society has submitted an application to the State of Hawaii for non-profit status through our attorney on this matter, Valentina Stewart. The paperwork for IRS 501c3 designation is in the process of being completed and will be filed within the next few weeks.

In the meantime, the Lahaina Open Space Society is accepting contributions through Maui Tomorrow.

The battle for Keka'a is at a critical stage, and all donations, at this time, are immensely appreciated.

Make your checks payable to Maui Tomorrow with a note at the bottom designating it for use by the Lahaina Open Space Society. Mail your checks to our treasurer and vice president, Sherri Carden, PO Box 102, Lahaina, HI 96767-0102. She'll make sure it is properly processed.

◆◆◆◆◆

Bumper stickers available

Save Keka'a bumper stickers are now available.

It's our first fund-raiser. ***So buy one!*** The cost is only $2.

Send us your check made out to the Lahaina Open Space Society, P. O. Box 102, Lahaina, HI 96767, and we'll send you one.

Thanks to Dave Tucker at Maui Printing and Kirk Apel at Surf Riders for helping us with this one!

Senate Bill 1021

In 1993 Senate Bill 1021 was introduced by U.S. Senator Daniel Inouye (D-HI).

This bill, 'To assure religious freedom to Native Americans,"is a very crucial piece of the re-emergence of Native American Indigenous Society. All Native Americans (including Native Hawaiians) should be knowledgable about it. Besides Senator Inouye, sponsors and support are both needed so that this law will not be rendered toothless by the usual opponents. Native American spiritual interests require special recognition. That they are the subject of legislation such as this, in order to preserve fundamental human rights such as those enjoyed by the mainstream entities in this society, speaks volumes on the state of affairs today. The Indian Canyon Community asks that you read this bill and urge Senators and Representatives to support it to the maximum extent possible."

According to Senator Inouye's office in Washington, the bill is currently in the committee, Committee on Indian and Native Hawaiian Affairs. We encourage you to write Inouye, who is the chair of this committee, to insure this legislation is passed on behalf of preserving religious sites for Native Hawaiians. You can find a full copy of Senate Bill 1021 on the internet:

http://hanksville.phast.umass.edu:80/misc/Senate1021.html.

Senator Inouye's address in Washington is: Senator Daniel Inouye, 722 Hart Senate Office Building, Washington D.C. 20510-1102.

Send a copy of your letter to all our state representatives in Washington: Senator Dan Akaka, 720 Hart Senate Office Building, Washington DC 20510-1103; Representative Patsy Mink, 2135 Rayburn Office Building, Washington DC 20515-1102; and Representative Neil Abercrombie, 1440

Longworth Office Building, Washington DC 20515-1101. Be sure to address your letter as follows: Honorable Senator Inouye.

◆◆◆◆◆◆◆◆◆◆

Earth Maui Nature Summit

The Lahaina Open Space Society will be participating in the 2nd Annual Earth Maui Nature Summit on August 30 at the Ritz-Carlton, Kapalua.

Sherri Carden will be unveiling a special painting of Keka'a, our vision for the site, that was painted by the children of our community.

Information on Lahaina Open Space Society, membership applications and the cultural significance of Keka'a will be available. Bumper Stickers will also be on sale.

Please stop by and visit our exhibit. Hours on the 30th are from 9 a.m. to 3 p.m.

◆◆◆◆◆◆◆◆◆◆

Keka'a seen as National Park

On Feb. 4, U.S. Rep. Patsy Mink introduced a bill to authorize a feasibility study that could make Keka'a a part of the National Park system. It was referred to the Committee on Resources, where the Subcommittee on National Parks and Public Lands failed to consider it. But in June, Mink made another push for the bill to be heard and has encouraged all interested persons to write the subcommittee chairman to "urge his consideration."

The National Park Service is not interested in beach parks, however, support for consideration of the purchase of Keka'a will be considered if the site has significance culturally, historically or naturally, which it does.

Please write Patsy Mink at the address we have previously listed. Also send a letter to the following Subcommittee Chairman in support of H.R. 576: The Honorable James V. Hansen, Chairman, Subcommittee on National Parks and Public Lands, H1-814 O'Neill House Office Building, Washington DC 20515.

Letters to the editor

At our last Lahaina Open Space Society meeting, it was agreed that Letters to the Editor sent to the various Maui newspapers have educated the community about our cause.

We encourage you to write one. The pen is mightier than the sword.

Fax numbers to the various newspapers are as follows: Lahaina News, 667-2726; Maui News, 242-9087; and Haleakala Times, 572-0168.

Write on!

Kaanapali Ocean Resort development status

What is the current status of Keka'a in the local application process for its development?

Since our last newsletter in April much has happened. A timeline of events (in approximate chronological order) is as follows:

* AMFAC submitted to the Maui Planning Commission three applications: (1) The proposed action involves the development of a vacation timeshare resort of up to 280 units, as well as related improvements and amenities; (2) The proposed request relates to Condition No. 7 concerning traffic mitigation for the Kaanapali North Beach Subdivision and involves widening Honoapiilani Highway to 4 lanes from Kaanapali Parkway to Honokowai Stream; and (3) The shoreline setback design guideline for the entire North Beach subdivision.

* Maui Planning Commission sets Public Hearing for July 10 at Lahaina Intermediate School.

* Jim and JoAnne Johnson, Buck Buchanan, Randy Draper, and Elizabeth and Dave Chenoweth filed legal documents to intervene on issues number 1 and number 2 above.

* The Maui County Council passes Resolution 97-147 making the following recommendations to the Maui Planning Commission: To conduct a publicly-noticed site inspection of Keka'a; to consider the potential impacts of the proposed development; and to consider the tremendous inadequacy of public park space in the West Maui region.

· Mayor Linda Lingle presents to the Maui County Council Land Use Committee a proposal to purchase 33 acres of the North Beach Subdivision as park space.

* At the July 10 Maui Planning Commission Hearing at Lahaina Intermediate School the intervenors were granted permissive intervention. The dispute will now be heard in a judicial setting with qualified experts giving sworn testimony subject to cross-examination by the hearing officer. Lawyer Isaac Davis Hall will be representing the intervenors.

* On Monday, August 11th, the Maui Planning Commission went on a site visit to Keka'a. From 7:30 to 9:30 a.m., the site visit was limited to the hearing officer, members of the Planning Commission, representatives of the intervenors, AMFAC and invited guests. At 9:30, the meeting was open to the public for comments and testimony.

* On Monday, August 18, the County Council considered a Resolution supporting the acquisition of approximately 33 acres of North Beach for park purposes. Resolution sent to Budge and Finance Committee for further discussion.

* Legal processes are ongoing culminating in the private contested case hearing to be held sometime in late September or early October after which the hearing officer will make recommendations to the Planning Commission and a decision will be rendered shortly thereafter.

◆◆◆◆◆◆◆◆◆◆

Much mahalos

The Lahaina Open Space Society owes a great debt of gratitude to intervenors Jim and JoAnne Johnson, Randy Draper, Buck Buchanan and Elizabeth and Dave Chenoweth.

Also Kudos to the Sierra Club for their kokua in assisting with our legal fund.

Huge hugs to our many contributors, both great and small, who believe in our mission to save Keka'a.

Lahaina Open Space Society 1 year old

Remember when people said, ***It's a done deal***, and ***you're crazy*** to think Keka'a can be saved for the community?

It was just one year ago on August 20, at Kahekili Park (at the south end of North Beach) that the Lahaina Open Space Society was formed at sunset. Buck Buchanan, Sherri Carden, Dave Chenoweth, Jackie Lee and Louise Rockett were there. Unable to attend were Randy Draper and Patty Nishiyama.

Determined to continue with our efforts (efforts which began during the community planning process) to save Keka'a, open space and culturally significant areas on the West Side, we considered Kahekili Park an auspicious place for our beginning.

In just one year, our numbers have increased significantly. Now the idea of saving Keka'a has spread throughout the community and across the country to Washington DC. The Mayor, the County Council, and Patsy Mink are all considering seriously the purchase of this last open space shoreline on the West Side and culturally significant area of Keka'a. Join us! We're not so crazy!

VOTE NO !!!
ON
CON CON

Concerns over development at Keka'a included the almost certain discovery of archaeological remains during construction, the increased traffic flow that would follow development of this area, the presence of wetlands on site, the need for wetland and water run-off structures and their ensuing impact on the shoreline and ocean environments, the growth in the local population and the lack of any existing or planned affordable housing for the entire area, and the obvious strain that further development would put on all public services (fire, police, electrical, water, waste, etc). All of these issues sparked debates on the growth of West Maui as a whole, and varying visions for that growth.

Since Keka'a was once a burial site, finding human remains there was virtually certain. Iwi kūpuna (ancestral bones) had been found at other nearby properties during development. For instance, "monitoring of construction work along the beachfront at the site of the Kaanapali Alii Condominiums did confirm the presence of prehistoric burials (Dobyns and Allen-Wheeler 1982)."[192] Another archaeological project had uncovered human bones during hotel construction in nearby Hanakao'o.[193]

Keka'a itself contains sand dunes, typically used as burial internment sites in Hawai'i, but previous archaeological surveys only uncovered a few agricultural remnants. In 1977, for

---

192 Peter M. Jensen, *Archaeological Inventory Survey Lahaina Master Planned Project Site, Land of Wahikuli, Lahaina District, Island of Maui*, October 1989, 5.

193 Helber, Hastert, and Kimura, *North Beach Kaanapali Final Environmental Impact Statement*, "Subsurface Archaeological Reconnaissance Survey," 5.

instance, for "the North Beach Mauka and South Beach Mauka project areas (involving c. 240 acres), Robert Hommon identified only three sites, including a simple agricultural complex and two short wall segments."[194]

Ten years later in 1987, Dr. Paul H. Rosendahl conducted a subsurface archaeological reconnaissance survey, and did not find anything substantial. The Environmental Impact Statement stated:

> In summary, the subsurface coring of the coastal dune did not identify any subsurface prehistoric cultural deposit or any human skeletal remains. The backhoe trenches and the soil profiles found no evidence of any cultural activities other than present cultivation of the land. One surface archaeological site, an L-shaped wall, was identified. However, this site has been evaluated as having minimal significance, and no further work is recommended for this feature. The findings suggest either there was little to no prehistoric use of the area, or that the evidence of prehistoric use is no longer present.[195]

Due to this lack of any significant archaeological finds at Keka'a, the final recommendations allowed construction to commence, but only under the supervision of an on-site archaeologist during the excavation of the sand dunes. This

194 Peter M. Jensen, *Archaeological Inventory Survey Lahaina Master Planned Project Site*, 5.

195 Helber, Hastert, and Kimura, *North Beach Kaanapali Draft Environmental Impact Statement*, V-7.

provision was emphasized because even though the land had been cleared for sugar cane cultivation and the Ka'anapali Airport, "there is still a possibility of isolated burials and/or remnants of buried cultural deposits within the project area."[196] It was also recommended that a stop-work policy be implemented with any discovery.[197] As explained in the Final Environmental Impact Statement, a staff of five or six persons canvassed the area, and collected 60 cores, with ten backhoe trenches used in the excavation. After the digging was completed, one new archaeological site was marked, but deemed not significant.[198]

Where were all the traces of Hawaiian communities? Even though taro terraces, petroglyphs, and iwi kūpuna were found across the Lahaina district, archaeologists have found relatively few remains of Hawaiian culture for the entire West Maui region. This should not be entirely surprising, since sugar plantations and hotel construction had already cleared the land, so many hints of prior settlement of human existence were destroyed. As noted in the reports, this presence caused "extensive surface

---

196 Helber, Hastert, and Kimura, *North Beach Kaanapali Final Environmental Impact Statement*, "Subsurface Archaeological Reconnaissance Survey," 22.

197 Helber, Hastert, and Kimura, *North Beach Kaanapali Draft Environmental Impact Statement*, V-7.

198 Helber, Hastert, and Kimura, *North Beach Kaanapali Final Environmental Impact Statement*, "Subsurface Archaeological Reconnaissance Survey," 1. Coring refers to the use of hand-powered corers that "extract from the earth soil cores 20 cm long and 10 cm in diameter....Detailed soil descriptions indicating location, microenvironmental setting, and adjacent vegetation were recorded for each core." (5 &6).

disturbance to which much of West Maui has been subjected by both resort development as well as historic and contemporary agricultural activities."[199]

Sugar cane production in particular had dramatically transformed not only the socio-economic realm, but in a more direct and violent manner, plowed through the landscape so that whatever remnants of Hawaiian culture remained were no longer visible. Following closely behind sugar production, the hotel developers did not need to invent a new social narrative of this land, but simply to build on the narrative of theft already enacted by the sugar growers—one that viewed ʻāina as empty space. The lack of cultural artifacts is further noted in the Archaeological Survey of North Beach:

> Previous archaeological work has also documented that much of the land located to the north of Lahaina has been extensively disturbed by historic and contemporary cane and pineapple cultivation. As a consequence of this disturbance, archaeological surveys of even relatively large parcels have occasionally failed to identify any resources at all. Based on these previous results, after reviewing aerial photographs and other project area maps, and in consideration of the fact that nearly 90% of the parcel has been subjected to intensive agricultural development, it was

199 Peter M. Jensen, *Archaeological Inventory Survey Lahaina Master Planned Project Site*, 5.

> considered likely that relatively few intact cultural properties would be encountered within the present project area.[200]

This absence was also noted for the larger West Maui area:

> Conspicuously absent from the present project area are major platforms or heiau features, and prehistoric-era trails. Proposed additional research (vegetation clearing in particular) at some of the gulch sites may reveal examples of the latter, although it is likely that the early historic agricultural clearing destroyed all of the large platform or heiau sites which may once have existed.[201]

What is destroyed cannot be recovered. Each new development reduced human relationships to land from dynamic and interactive to one-dimensional matters of capital. In this social narrative, entitlements of the developers were prioritized.

The silence of the landscape is telling, as the clearing and rebuilding of the canvas continues. By 1996, the absence of cultural artifacts was identified as an overall epistemological lacking:

> In terms of cultural resources, preliminary research of reference materials relating to Maui and the Kaanapali area indicated that there is no evidence that the project site in particular has any historic significance to native Hawaiians. A

---

200 Peter M. Jensen, *Archaeological Inventory Survey Lahaina Master Planned Project Site*, 6.

201 Peter M. Jensen, *Archaeological Inventory Survey Lahaina Master Planned Project Site*, 26.

study of mo'olelo (stories) dealing with Maui and the Kaanapali area revealed that there is no indication that the project site itself has any mythological significance. In addition, based on conversations with representatives of present day native Hawaiian families residing in the Kaanapali area, there is no evidence that the project site is regarded as important for religious, subsistence, or health purposes (personal communication from George Kanahele, George S. Kanahele & Associates, May 1996). [202]

The idea of "no significance" was further exemplified in the 1996 Application for Special Management Area Use Permit. Bolded, with subheadings to follow, each point was laid bare:

1. **There is no evidence, either in documentary or oral (chant) material, that the project site has any historic, traditional or neo-traditional, significance.**
2. **There is no mythological evidence that the project site has any significance, although there are significant legends concerning the larger surrounding area of Ka'anapali.**
3. **There is no archaeological evidence, based on previous archaeological investigations, that the project site was or is a culturally important site.**
4. **There is no evidence that the site is of traditional importance to Hawaiian families residing in the**

202 Munekiyo and Arakawa, Inc., *Final Environmental Assessment (EISPN), Kaanapali Vacation Club*, August 1996, 26.

surrounding area for either religious, health or totally subsistence purposes. [203]

Like some perverse development mantra, "no evidence and no significance" was drummed into the documents and through its inclusion reinforced that idea that the land is disconnected from the surrounding environment. Here the landscape was systematically flattened of significance so that a re-imagination of the space could occur—one that ignored larger land narratives. And in this flattened state, more immediate concerns would be addressed. At the forefront was that the installation of what was projected to be another Ka'anapali would multiply the strain on an already stretched West Maui infrastructure—including the exponential use of public services like water, waste, fire, police, and other county services.

At the top of the list of concerns was traffic congestion. Only one road goes in and out of the Ka'anapali area, the same road that connects West Maui to the rest of the island. How would locals and visitors navigate more traffic on the already congested Honoapi'ilani Highway? In 1987, it was declared that the North Beach development would be completed in 1994, so the traffic analysis in the EIS was projected for that year. In 1987, the traffic count for the area had ranged from between 26,800 to 37,500 vehicles traveling between Lahaina and Ka'anapali a day. This

203 Munekiyo and Arakawa, Inc., *Final Environmental Assessment (EISPN), Kaanapali Vacation Club*, 37-40.

number was projected to increase to 40,985 vehicles per day in 1994 *without* the North Beach project:[204]

> The traffic projections without the proposed project were developed for the target year 1994 which would have been the date of completion for the North Beach Kaanapali Resort.
>
> South of Kaanapali, the northbound lane of Honoapiilani Highway would be over capacity with V/C ratio of 1.37. The southbound lanes operate at a VC ratio of 0.83. The intersection of Honoapiilani Highway and Kaanapali Parkway would be over capacity. Honoapiilani Highway, north of Kaanapali Parkway, would be over capacity with a V/C ratio of 1.1.
>
> The intersection of Honoapiilani and Puukolii Road/Kai Ala Drive would be over capacity due to the increase in through traffic on Honoapiilani Highway. North of Puukolii Road/Kai Ala Drive, Honoapiilani Highway would be near capacity with a V/C ratio of 0.98.
>
> By the year 1990, the northbound lane of Honoapiilani Highway, south of Kaanapali, would be over capacity with a V/C ratio of 1.06. The southbound lanes would operate at a ratio of 0.82. The intersection of Honoapiilani Highway and Kaanapali Parkway would be over capacity primarily due to the heavy left turn demand from Honoapiilani Highway, northbound, to Kaanapali Parkway conflicting with through traffic on

---

204 Helber, Hastert, and Kimura, *North Beach Kaanapali Final Environmental Impact Statement*, "Environmental Impact Analysis," V-8 & V-9.

Honoapiilani Highway, southbound. This would be a worsening of the existing capacity conditions. [205]

These traffic projections would give any West Maui resident reason enough to be concerned. Adding to the grim statistics were the suggested three stages of road development that would coincide with the North Beach development—grim, because the projections relied primarily on a Bypass Highway from Lahaina to the Ka'anapali area that was many, many years from development and actual completion.

Besides road widening and traffic signal coordination, the building and completion of the Lahaina Bypass Highway will one day eventually provide an alternate route and help to facilitate Honoapi'ilani Highway. At present, it is still not completed. In July 1988, Condition No. 7 was included in the Special Management Area Permit (SMA) for the North Beach Subdivision.[206] Continued development of West Maui was not to be initiated without the completion of this Bypass Highway or "other mitigating measures." Defining "other mitigating measures" as a simple expansion of the already present two-lane highway to four lanes

205 Helber, Hastert, and Kimura, *North Beach Kaanapali Final Environmental Impact Statement*, "Traffic Impact Report for the Proposed North Beach Kaanapali Resort Development," August 1987, 15 & 18.

206 *Contested Case Hearing: September 22, 1997-October 3, 1997.* Findings of Fact, Conclusions of Law, Decision and Order, Nos. 88/SM1-023, 88/SSV-002, and SM1 970006. County of Maui, State of Hawai'i, October 28, 1988.

would be a fight recorded in the development documents for many years to come.

In 1987, the expedient building of the Bypass Highway and the coordination and building of its connecting transportation infrastructure was given an unrealistic completion date of 1992:

> The traffic conditions projected for 1992 would require the construction of a two-lane, high quality Bypass Highway beginning at Puamana, south of Lahaina, to Honokowai, north of Kaanapali. The Bypass Highway is being planned by the State DOT at this writing. Although the alignment and financing have not been determined at this writing, a "fast-track" 1992 completion date is considered feasible. The Bypass Highway should also include connector roads leading down to Honoapiilani Highway to collect and distribute local traffic as well as allow through traffic to bypass Lahaina and Kaanapali. [207]
>
> The SDOT-proposed Bypass Highway and four lane widening of Honoapiilani Highway, implemented in a timely manner, and the proposed improvements recommended in this study, should mitigate the traffic impacts resulting from this project and the overall growth of West Maui. [208]

And then a few years later:

---

207 Helber, Hastert, and Kimura, *North Beach Kaanapali Final Environmental Impact Statement*, "Traffic Impact Report for the Proposed North Beach Kaanapali Resort Development," 22.

208 Helber, Hastert, and Kimura, *North Beach Kaanapali Final Environmental Impact Statement*, "Traffic Impact Report for the Proposed North Beach Kaanapali Resort Development," v.

> The Hawaii State Department of Transportation plans to construct a four-lane highway bypass from Launiupoko to Honokowai to alleviate traffic congestion on Honoapiilani Highway. The project is scheduled to begin in late 1994 and be complete by 1996 or 1997, contingent on State purchase of the West Maui Airport and related financing for the highway improvements.[209]

The Bypass Highway was not completed. Even Amfac recognized that temporary mitigative measures would not effectively control traffic, and that the Bypass was indeed a necessity for this region. In 1996, Teney Takahashi, Senior Vice President at Amfac wrote:

> Let me emphasize however, that Amfac Maui is not suggesting that the widening is a permanent substitute for the bypass. Amfac is committed to the bypass. We have already spent a total of $1.1 million of our $3.5 million commitment on the bypass, and we will not jeopardize this investment in the highway system that we need for our Puukolii project and Kaanapali projects. It would serve neither the community nor Amfac to delay the bypass. [210]

By 1997, the North Beach development had been delayed eleven years by the intervenors based on many concerns, including increased traffic for the area. "Intervenors" was the name given to a community group by the Maui Planning Commission in 1997 based on its attempt to intervene in the North

209 PBR Hawaii, *Final Environmental Impact Report, Puukolii Village, Volume II,* 3-3

210 Teney K. Takahashi, Amfac Senior Vice President, *Amfac Letter*, December 26, 1996.

Beach development of Lot 1. They were tagged "conservationists versus the developers" because they very clearly had a "no development" stance in regards to Keka'a.[211] Among this group were James and Jo Anne Johnson Winer, Randy Draper, Robert "Buck" Buchanan, and David and Elizabeth Chenoweth.

In July 1997, the *Lahaina News* reported, "After a long public hearing last week Thursday, the Maui Planning Commission decided to allow Robert H. Buchanan, Randy Draper and James and Joanne Johnson Winer to intervene on two matters linked to North Beach."[212] This same newspaper article quoted longtime Maui councilman Wayne Nishiki as saying "As elected officials we have not done a good job for the West Side community. I am embarrassed. This is the last sandy beach to preserve."[213] Nishiki, an organic farmer for decades, was known on Maui as being the voice of the community in local government.

The 1997 intervention wanted to review a Special Management Area Permit by Amfac that would lead to a 280-unit condominium on Lot 1 of North Beach—the first development to proceed. Multiple issues were tackled in this intervention, with the primary one being a review of Condition No. 7, which centered on the Lahaina Bypass Highway. As a result of the intervention, a contested case hearing ran from September

211 Mark A. Howland, Chief Biologist, Environmental Research Corps. "Can North Beach Be Saved?," 1997.

212 Mark Veith, "North Beach Issues to be Dissected in Lengthy Hearings," *Lahaina News*, Vol. 18, No. 29, July 17-July 23, 1997, p. 1.

213 Mark Veith, "North Beach Issues to be Dissected in Lengthy Hearings," 2.

22, 1997 to October 3, 1997. This case put specific conditions in place that would control the magnitude of the development, including the implementation of a shoreline setback ordinance of 150 feet for the entirety of the North Beach property, the proclamation of open space and community park land, and an interpretation of Condition No. 7. Condition No. 7 declares that:

> Prior to the commencement of the operation of the initial project to be constructed within the North Beach subdivision, the Lahaina Bypass Highway or other mitigative measures or terms, as approved by the Planning Commission, shall be implemented.[214]

The *Lahaina News* explained:

> The condition factored heavily into Amfac's plans, because if the bypass requirement is kept, developers can't start projects at North Beach until the bypass—a traffic feeder road from Lahaina to Honokowai—is built. The roadway has been delayed for years in design, and completion of the four-lane bypass is probably 10 to 20 years away, state officials said.[215]

Since construction of the Lahaina Bypass Highway was many, many years away, and today is still years away from completion, the question became what "other mitigative measures or terms"

---

214 Joel E. August, *Contested Case Hearing: September 22, 1997-October 3, 1997*, Nos. 88/SM1-0123, 88/SSV-002 and SM 970006., Hearing Officer's Report with Proposed Findings of Fact and Conclusions of Law, Decision and Order, 5.

215 Mark Veith, "Mayor and Council Discuss Stances on North Beach," *Lahaina News*, Vol. 18, No. 28, July 10-July 16, 1997, p. 1.

might be. Development hinged on a favorable interpretation of this clause. Amfac declared that widening the two-lane road to four-lanes would fulfill this traffic requirement. The no-development community sector disagreed, with hundreds coming out to testify against the development. This in turn led to the contested court case for further clarification.

Caught up in this mix was also an offer put forth by Mayor Linda Lingle for the county to purchase over 30 acres of North Beach for open space preservation. This purchase would factor favorably into the overall development of North Beach, since it would contribute to a decrease in condominium units, and therefore provide relief from traffic congestion and the overall impact of any development. This deal assured the public that a four-lane highway would suffice as a "mitigative measure" because then a third of the area of North Beach would not be developed. Condition No. 7 was therefore seen to be satisfied. The *Lahaina News* reported:

> Mayor Linda Crockett Lingle, meanwhile, told council members the county had been negotiating an agreement with Amfac Maui to buy and preserve 30 acres at North Beach for $15 million.
>
> Speaking in terms of the possible pact with Amfac, Mayor Lingle said the county will agree the highway widening can accommodate the traffic generated by the time share. In turn, Amfac will sell the county 30 acres at the north end of North

Beach for $15 million and reduce the density of the entire subdivision from 3,200 to 2,000 units.[216]

The *Haleakalā Times* wrote:

> Lingle proposed spending $15 million to buy 33 acres of the North Beach site for public park use. That acreage reportedly has been appraised at $41 million. In return for its bargain buy on the parkland, the county would drop its insistence that any North Beach development must await completion of the long-promised 'Lahaina Bypass' state highway.
>
> Envisioned 20 years ago as a 1990s mauka thoroughfare that would relieve traffic congestion between Lahaina and Honokowai, the Lahaina Bypass now has been pushed back at least a decade by state fiscal shortfalls and other factors. Any such bypass would require state acquisition of a multi-million dollar corridor through Pioneer Mill sugar property owned by Amfac.
>
> The mayor said repeatedly that the administration would waive the by-pass requirement only for the first of several proposed Amfac/JMB developments at North Beach.[217]

The Maui News wrote:

> The tentative deal involves more than just a swap of cash for beachfront land, Lingle said.

---

216 Veith, Mark, "Mayor and Council Discuss Stances on North Beach, p. 1.

217 Tom Stevens, "West Maui—AMFAC's North Beach; condos a-comin, Lingle calls Patsy Mink's North Beach park proposal 'hollow,'" *Haleakalā Times,* July 16-August 5, 1997, p.1 & 6.

> Amfac also would agree to reduce the overall density of North Beach hotel development from 3,200 to about 2,000 units.
>
> In return, the mayor would quit resisting Amfac's request for a favorable interpretation of condition No. 7 on its special management area permit.[218]

Another *The Maui News* article reported:

> The question of whether the county Department of Corporation Counsel can provide unbiased advice arises from an agreement giving Maui County an option to pay $15 million for a 33.8-acre park at North beach, also known as Kekaa.
>
> The pact, signed Sept. 22 by Mayor Linda Lingle and approved in form and legality by Corporation Counsel J.P. Schmidt, calls for the county immediately to fully support developer Amfac's application for special management area permit for the 280-unit Kaanapali Ocean Resort.[219]

And finally:

> The controversy climaxed last September when it was revealed that Mayor Linda Lingle and key administration officials had signed a pact with the developers that would allow the county to buy a third of the area for $15 million, in exchange for their support of the project, which would be scaled back from 3,200 units to 1,950.

---

218 Harry Eager, "North Beach deal could be in the making: Council hears from mayor on idea to buy one-third of property," *The Maui News*, July 8, 1997.

219 Brian Perry, "Panel balks at action on North Beach, Question raised on objectivity of county lawyers," *The Maui News*, October 29, 1997, 1.

> Because Corporation Counsel J.P. Schmidt drafted the option-to-purchase agreement, causing a possible conflict of interest for county attorneys, the Planning Commission asked for [Jon] Van Dyke to serve as special counsel.[220]

Besides turning into an apparent conflict of interest debacle, the contested case hearing for North Beach came back with what for some was a joint victory for the developers and the community when the hearing officer, Joel E. August, recommended that the construction permit be approved, but with some conditions.[221] August approved the development of Lot 1 at Keka'a by recognizing that the four-lane implementation does fulfill Condition No. 7. August dealt with Condition No. 7 and the land swap—now 38.8 acres of open space— by stating that the swap should be in place before Phase II. He also clarified that the development would commence in three phases.

> The Commission concludes that the language in Condition 7 is not ambiguous. By its own terms it provides the Commission with authority to approve traffic mitigation measures other than the Lahaina Bypass Highway should the Highway not be in place prior to the opening of the initial project at North Beach.
>
> The next step in any analysis is to determine whether the proposed expansion of Honoapiilani Highway between

---

220 Valerie Monson, "North Beach struggle put on shelf for a month: Parties to SMA permit case look for agreement," *The Maui News*, May 13, 1998, A3.

221 Mark Veith, "Hearing officer recommends approval for new time share at North Beach," *Lahaina News*, Vol. 19, No. 2, January 8-January 14, 1998, 1.

> Kaanapali Parkway and Honokowai Stream, and related intersection improvements, would be appropriate mitiagative measures in light of the evidence presented during the contested case hearing and in light of the policies and objectives contained in H.R.S. Chapter 205. The Commission concludes that such improvements would be adequate to address the traffic impacts created by the Kaanapali Ocean Resort development and that they would be consistent with the CZMA policies and objectives.
>
> (And listed in the conditions) Construction of a public beach park of not less than 38.8 acres at North Beach must be commenced prior to a certificate of occupancy being issued for phase II of the Kaanapali Ocean Resort Development.[222]

Also proposed was Congresswoman Patsy Mink's attempt to preserve open space. She drafted House Resolution (H.R.) 576 to the U.S. Congress in hopes of saving North Beach as a National Park. H.R. 576 wrote up North Beach as one of four areas up for National Park recognition in Hawai'i. The others were Hale, the mountaintop area on Lana'i, the shoreline area from Anini Beach to Makua Tunnels on Kaua'i, and Halawa Valley on Moloka'i.[223] Patsy Mink wrote to the Chair of the U.S. House Resources Subcommittee on National Parks and Public Lands:

> I strongly urge approval of H.R. 576 by your subcommittee. It is important to fully understand the appropriateness of putting

222 Joel E. August, 39 & 43.

223 Patsy Mink, H.R. 576, 105th Congress, 1st Session, "To direct the Secretary of the Interior to undertake the necessary feasibility studies regarding the establishment of certain new units of the National Park System in the State of Hawaii."

four of Hawaii's few remaining open spaces and culturally sensitive areas under the care, protection and management of the U.S. Department of the Interior, rather than leaving them to be built over by encroaching development.[224]

This Resolution was not passed. Maui Planning Commissioner Joe Bertram suggested acquiring all of the North Beach property and "the sugar lands mauka of that property for a Hawaiian botanical and cultural preserve."[225] And, Wayne Nishiki proposed a Resolution to the County Council "Supporting the Acquisition of Approximately 33 acres at North Beach for Park Purposes." None of these initiatives ever materialized. After all this negotiating over securing a large stretch of open space, development continued without this concession.

In 1996, David W. Blane, the Director of Planning for Maui County, wrote the following letter to John Akana, Chair, and Members for the Maui Planning Commission:

> Please consider this letter as an addendum to the Director's Report dated December 10, 1996, regarding Amfac Maui's request to have the widening of Honoapiilani Highway considered as a mitigative measure for the proposed construction of their Kaanapali Vacation Club. At this time, I would like to inform the Commissioners that the Planning Department does not feel that

224 Letter from Patsy T. Mink to The Honorable James V. Hansen, Chair House Resources Subcommittee on National Parks and Public Lands, June 5, 1997.

225 Tom Stevens, 6.

the proposal constitutes adequate mitigative measures and, therefore, does not support this request.

After reviewing the lengthy history of this issue, it is clear to me that the Lahaina Bypass was always considered a necessity before any North Beach hotels could be built. The thread of this assumption winds through all the subsequent approvals including the West Maui Community Plan that was adopted by the Council on February 27, 1996. Although detailed traffic calculations may show that the proposed widening of this section of Honoapiilani Highway may address the short-term traffic impacts of this hotel, the Department must evaluate this proposal over the **long term**.

Although the decision is up to the Maui Planning Commissioners, I hope that you will consider what appears to be the clear intent of the original conditions for North Beach and that was that the Lahaina Bypass be completed.

Thank you for your consideration of my recommendation.

Very Truly yours,
David W. Blane
Director of Planning[226]

Widening of the Highway was apparently deemed enough, but it was not an idea necessarily embraced by any stakeholders other than the developers. The developers had other suggestions for easing traffic congestion—water ferries, providing hotel employee carpooling, expanding airport shuttle bus services, and a jitney service, which would presumably include a park-

226 Letter from David W. Blane to John Akana, Chair and Members Maui Planning Commission. Re: Kaanapali North Beach Joint Venture, December 6, 1996.

and-ride and ride-sharing program.[227] Renting cars by the hour, rental car incentive programs, and a water route between Lahaina and Ka'anapali rounded out the suggestions proposed as part of the massive development plans for North Beach.

The planners also hoped to "require change in people's behavior, i.e., encouraging HOV use and discouraging single-person driving." And "to further encourage auto-less transportation, the development should incorporate a scale of urban and landscaping design compatible with safe and enjoyable pedestrian and bicycle movement."[228] Where did the developers think they were living? Or, perhaps more key, where did they think they were planning, and who were they planning for? The planners probably were not living near the area, whereas most hotel workers have to commute across the island to get to work, work long hours at sometimes two or three hotel jobs, and then drive home: "With housing limited, many who work in West Maui live upcountry or in central Maui and commute 40 miles or more each workday."[229] Carpooling and commuter buses are often impractical, due to different shifts and extended work hours. Tourists also have to commute to and from the international airport located in Kahului, on the only

227 Helber, Hastert, and Kimura, *North Beach Kaanapali Final Environmental Impact Statement*, v.

228 Helber, Hastert, and Kimura, *North Beach Kaanapali Final Environmental Impact Statement*, "North Beach Transportation Study," 16.

229 Helber, Hastert, and Kimura, *Final Environmental Impact Report, Puukolii Village, Volume II*, 2-12.

road in and out of West Maui. "Auto-less transportation" might only be doable *after* you get to your West Maui destination.

Development of the entire area—North Beach, Pu'ukoli'i, and other developments—still awaits the completion of the Bypass Highway. Some development has occurred, while other projects have not. According to Jo Anne Johnson Winer, the current Director of the Maui Department of Transportation and one of the original intervenors in North Beach Lot 1, the 1990s agreement was no development of North Beach until the Bypass Highway was completed. Settlements in the 2000s between Amfac and other intervenors changed this; half of the first intervenors had left the case by the final settlement phase of Lot 1, and so this deal was signed by a few of the intervenors, their lawyer, Isaac Hall, and the developers.

Today the Lahaina Bypass Highway is still under construction and will not be completed until at least 2018.[230] The North Beach planners were therefore at least twenty-six years off in their estimation of a 1992 completion date. North Beach is now mostly built without the shops, hospitals, day-care services, parks, and other planned amenities, since "Easy access to the Lahaina Bypass Highway will also make travel to work or shopping more convenient than it is from many current neighborhoods."[231]

---

230 Interview with Jo Anne Johnson Winer, Director of Transportation, Maui County, January 18, 2013.

231 Helber, Hastert, and Kimura, *Final Environmental Impact Report, Puukolii Village, Volume II*, 4-5.

Another major infrastructure concern with Keka'a was that a portion lies in a wetland area. Trying to control these waters, and the run-off from higher elevations onto this area, would result in building structures that would negatively impact shoreline and ocean environments. The original plan for drainage called for a trapezoidal channel that would discharge waters through an outfall pipeline, terminating offshore.[232] But the Army Corps of Engineers was concerned that the drainage outfall would negatively impact water quality and the communities of coral located offshore.[233] A new 1987 plan eliminated the proposed outfall, and fed runoff from Hanakao'o Gulch and the agricultural lands between Hanakao'o Gulch and Pu'ukoli'i Road into one trapezoidal channel that discharged at the shoreline. The channel location was moved further south, away from the more prominent coral communities.[234] These measures were seen as beneficial steps in taming the wetland:

> The overall drainage impact resulting from elimination of the ocean outfall and relocation of the open channel should be positive. By removing the outfall, two impacts are eliminated: 1) the direct destruction of coral from outfall construction, and 2) the offshore discharge of freshwater and sediment near the

232 Helber, Hastert, and Kimura, *North Beach Kaanapali Final Environmental Impact Statement*, "North Beach Transportation Study," V-23.

233 Helber, Hastert, and Kimura, *North Beach Kaanapali Final Environmental Impact Statement*, "North Beach Transportation Study," V-23.

234 Helber, Hastert, and Kimura, *North Beach Kaanapali Final Environmental Impact Statement*, "North Beach Transportation Study," V-23.

> ocean bottom. The open channel and channel outlet will restore the natural outlet for Hanakaoo Gulch, the natural drainageway on the mauka side of Honoapiilani Highway. There will be four 12-foot wide box culverts to carry the water underground across Honoapiilani Highway to the site. The restoration of the direct outlet to the ocean will greatly reduce the likelihood of flooding of the area immediately below the gulch and of Honoapiilani Highway. The channelization of the water will result in higher velocity inflow to the ocean, and the storm water and associated sediment load will be taken quickly offshore rather than diffusely entering the nearshore areas.[235]
>
> The overall drainage impact will be positive. The open channel and channel outlet will restore the natural outlet for Hanakaoo Gulch, the natural drainageway on the mauka side of Honoapiilani Highway... The outfall will discharge storm water beyond the near shore areas of high quality coral growth, within a sandy bottom area. Negative impacts are primarily due to construction activity, including removal of some coral during construction of the outfall.[236]

The Application for a Special Management Area Use Permit for the Ka'anapali Ocean Resort—the first hotel slated to occupy Lot 1—documented the wetland issue. A shoreline setback area

235 Helber, Hastert, and Kimura, *North Beach Kaanapali Final Environmental Impact Statement*, "North Beach Transportation Study," V-25.

236 Dames and Moore, *Environmental Assessment for Department of the Army Permit Application, North Beach, Ka'anapali*, Kaanapali North Beach Joint Venture, June 10, 1987, 1.

was established in 1996; according to this report, "within the shoreline setback area is a wetland area."[237] It further explained:

> The wetland on the project site serves to provide drainage and sendimentation functions for storm water runoff originating from Kahekili Park and the Kai Ala Subdivision to the south.
>
> The wetland is situated within an area proposed for landscaping and recreational beachside uses. A Section 404 Permit from the department of the Army, as well as a Section 401 Water Quality Certification from the State Department of Health, and a Coastal Zone Management Consistency Review by the Office of State Planning will be required to fill the wetland.
>
> A wetland mitigation plan is being developed in coordination with the Department of the Army. The objective of the plan is to mitigate the drainage and sedimentation functions of the wetland. The mitigation proposal will be addressed in the EIS document.[238]

In other words, drying out the wetlands was necessary for development. Drainage was also addressed for the widening of Honoapi'ilani Highway because the runoff from the West Maui Mountains flowed onto then existing wetlands through

237 Munekiyo and Arakawa, Inc., Prepared for Amfac. *Application for Special Management Area Use Permit, Ka'anapali Ocean Resort*, March 1997, 48.

238 Helber, Hastert, and Kimura, *Final Environmental Assessment (EISPN), Kaanapali Vacation Club,* 31.

culverts passing under the Highway.[239] The fear for many was that drainage would negatively affect coral communities and the ocean environment.

In the 1990s, Chief Biologist Mark A. Howland wrote a report to the Planning Commission, opposing the developers. Howland had been hired by the intervenors to do a study of the wetlands. A big question at the time was why development was even being allowed at all. Wetlands contribute to the biodiversity of the environment. The *Haleakalā Times* commented that "Wetlands and floodplains not only purify the waters that pass through them, eliminating toxins and debris, they also return these cleansed water to the aquifer, replenishing its supply. In water-starved Lahaina, this is important."

Howland emphasized the importance of wetlands in his 1997 report to the Maui Planning Commission. He noted that the SMA permit for the Ka'anapali Ocean Resorts "acknowledges the other wetlands areas on the site and says 'they may be permanent.' Why are not these areas considered wetlands if they have hydrology, vegetation, etc...? The Corps has no size limit on wetlands."[240] And, "'I counted six areas that are definitely wetlands,' said Howland, 'And there's four other areas that we

---

239 Austin, Tsutumi and Associates, Inc., *Drainage Report for the Honoapiilani Highway Widening Project*, Department of Transportation, Highways Division, State of Hawai'i, January, 1997, 6.

240 Mark A. Howland, Chief Biologist, Environmental Research Corps, *Commentary to the Maui Planning Commission in response to the proposed Ka'anapali Ocean Resorts by AMFAC Maui*, August 25, 1997, note 14, page 3.

need to take a closer look at to see if they qualify.'"[241] Howland is referring to the fact that although this area was documented as containing wetlands early on, this information was disregarded so that the lands could be developed, as if there were indeed *no* wetlands. Or perhaps the definition of how big a wetland must be to halt development was on a fluid scale. It is confusing, and only partly because the documents vacillate between *yes there are wetlands/no there are no wetlands* present.

Howland bluntly wrote "These are federal wetlands. There's no question that they're wetlands. So they (Amfac/JMB) shouldn't be doing a thing until they apply for a federal wetland permit."[242] The SMA responded that "Silt and debris will be removed and properly disposed of through periodic maintenance. The existing shoreline sand dune and wetland area will remain in their natural state."[243] Howland responded:

> Silt and debris removal is seldom done. A maintenance plan suggestion is seldom followed up on, and seldom enforced. The site owners already have a poor history of silt removal actions with the ocean now having silt plumes extending into the ocean. No corrective action is being done. Again this paragraph mentions the dune and shoreline and wetlands being left in natural state

---

241 Andrew Jacoby, "North Beach Venture hotel plans could be bogged down in wetlands," *Maui Tribune,* Vol. 1, Issue 18, April 12, 1995, p. 1 & 9.

242 Lucienne DeNaie, "The proposed new development at North Beach-Part 2: Environmental impacts and 'mitigation.'" *Haleakalā Times*, March 5-18, 1997, 6.

243 Munekiyo and Arakawa, Inc., *Application for Special Management Area Use Permit, Ka'anapali Ocean Resort*, 104.

> which contradicts the forested buffer being cut and trimmed and replaced by manicured landscapes, the wetlands functioning as runoff storage areas, and the dunes breached or covered with walkways. What natural state?[244]

Howland had other concerns about the development, such as the undocumented turtle nesting area, the runoff storage areas that were structures and therefore should not be allowed in the setback areas, and the prior evidence of Hawaiian burial sites and artifacts in the larger Keka'a area that were now being ignored. Howland finished his statement with "Banning the development is the best recommendation."[245]

Despite these concerns, Amfac's plans for Keka'a gained momentum in 1997 during Maui County planning hearings. The intervenors responded:

> The last break in the shoreline chain of development is North Beach. Site of the old Hawaiian capital of Keka'a, North Beach is the last large piece of undeveloped shore land left in West Maui. And now, using the banner of economy jump-starter, AMFAC Maui and its limited partnership, Ka'anapali Ownership Resorts L.P.; propose closing the last link of the shoreline development chain. They have proposed subdividing the land into four large lots, the first of which will house a 280 unit timeshare condominium complex next to the beach; and necessitate the

---

244 Howland, *Commentary to the Maui Planning Commission in response to the proposed Ka'anapali Ocean Resorts by AMFAC Maui,* note 42, p. 5-6.

245 Howland, *Commentary to the Maui Planning Commission in response to the proposed Ka'anapali Ocean Resorts by AMFAC Maui*, 8.

> widening of the Honoapiilani Highway from two lanes to four lanes to accommodate the planned increase of traffic.[246]
>
> The intervenors' group charged AMFAC with clearing vegetation, destroying sand dunes, and filling wetlands in order to hide or destroy some of the natural resources before review and permitting is made. For the record, AMFAC has denied these actions, but in June sent Draper a letter reminding him of their no trespass action taken against him, and warned him to stay away from the 'minor work related to the ongoing agricultural operations and harvesting' on the site.[247]

The intervenors' alleged that Amfac was cutting down trees, filling in the wetlands with tree cuttings, cutting through dunes, thinning the "forested buffer," and encouraging illegal camping—all to degrade and misrepresent the area. Further, "The runoff flows have been directed to the on-site acknowledged wetlands, to the chain of small wetland pockets along the back edge of the forested buffer, and into the ocean itself through man-made 'cuts' in the sand dune."[248] These environmental travesties did not jive with the intervenors' proposed vision "of open space and recreational park use with interpretive trails (that) seems to fit the site's need much better than another timeshare resort."[249]

Amfac responded to a letter documenting these

---

246 Howland, "Can North Beach Be Saved?" 2.

247 Howland, "Can North Beach Be Saved?" 3.

248 Howland, "Can North Beach Be Saved?" 5.

249 Howland, "Can North Beach Be Saved?" 7.

environmental travesties with their own May 30, 1997 letter to Jo Anne Johnson Winer and Randy Draper.

> Amfac and Tobishima Pacific, Inc. have reviewed a copy of your May 26, 1997 letter to the Maui County Council regarding 'Illegal North Beach tree/vegetation removal/wetland destruction.' The allegations contained in that letter are entirely false. Futhermore, it is obvious that you made absolutely no effort to determine whether your outrageous charges against Amfac and Tobishima were in the least bit accurate. There can be no doubt from the deliberately defamatory contents of the letter that it was calculated to mislead the Maui County Council and cause damage and harassment to Amfac and Tobishima at a time when they are seeking to develop a portion of their North Beach property.[250]

Jo Anne Johnson Winer and Randy Draper then requested a site visitation with the County Council so that they could see the area for themselves, adding that

> At that time, should you care to show which of the statements made in our communication to the County Council are false, deliberately defamatory, have caused damage, harassment and are misleading, we will be happy to correct and/or retract those statements.[251]

---

250 Letter from Teney K. Takahashi, Senior Vice President Amfac to Jo Anne Johnson Winer and Randy Draper, May 30, 1997.

251 Letter from Jo Anne Johnson Winer and Randy Draper to Teney K. Takahashi, June 4, 1997.

All of this occurred after the Maui County Council "walkaround" of North Beach on May 7, 1997, but another "walkaround" was requested by the intervenors. The fight was far from over, and on June 27, 1997, Amfac sent Randy Draper a letter warning him off the property:

> Dear Mr. Draper:
>
> This is in response to your letter of June 4, 1997. Please be advised that the purpose of our invitation to the Council is to demonstrate that none of the charges you made regarding damage to the wetlands, etc. is true. We have no obligation or need to include you or your associates in this discussion or excursion onto our property. In fact, the warning you and Mark Howland received on May 23, 1995 against trespassing still stands.
>
> I reiterate that we did not take part in any of the unsubstantiated allegations in your letter of May 26, 1997. It is therefore your responsibility to either prove otherwise, withdraw your unfounded accusations, or suffer appropriate consequences.
>
> Sincerely,
> Amfac Maui
> Teney K. Takahashi
> Senior Vice President[252]

252 Letter from Teney K. Takahashi to Randy Draper, June 27, 1997.

"Suffer appropriate consequences"—threats from Amfac peppered the correspondence and heightened the tension of the already contentious fight to save Keka'a. But developers did concede some points from the first North Beach Environmental Impact Statement: the donation of two public parks to the community, and the construction of an affordable housing project (that was required anyway) called Pu'ukoli'i. The parks attracted criticism because of their size and location:

> We have reviewed the Environmental Impact Statement (EIS) for the North Beach Project in Kaanapali on Maui.
>
> We have the following comments regarding the two sites that will be dedicated to the County of Maui for public park use.
>
> The proposed park lots are not acceptable. Lot 8 configuration is not suitable for a park and Lots 9, 10, or 11 are too small.
>
> We would prefer Lot 2 or Lot 3 be designated as the beach park as long as the grade is appropriate. Beach access should be retained at Lot 8 and at the South end.
>
> As an alternative, Lots 9, 10, 11 and a portion of Lot 1 could be combined to form a beach park of 6 to 10 acres and beach accesses retained between Lot 3 and Lot 4 and at Lot 8.
>
> We believe that the community will best be served with beach parks with adequate space requirements in a functional fashion.
>
> We understand the community plan land use designations

are set but we recommend that this designation be reviewed. Adequate beach front for public use should be retained.

Sincerely,
Marilyn Moniz-Kahoohanohano
Director of Parks & Recreation[253]

The developers wanted the parks located at opposite ends of the development so that the resort feel would be kept intact. "Heavy public access directly in and out of the resort could exacerbate traffic and parking problems, as well as create the public perception that the beach park 'belongs' to the resort, rather than to the community."[254] This giving back to the community, but only if the community is kept on the outer fringes of the development, was revised a few months later in the developer's response to Marilyn Moniz-Kaho'ohanohano: "Alternative park configurations, including the ones you have suggested, are being considered."[255]

The battle over Lot 1 was fought on all levels. Randy Draper, one of the first intervenors and an active member of the various

---

253 Helber, Hastert, and Kimura, *North Beach Kaanapali Final Environmental Impact Statement*, "Project Testimony," XII-32.

254 Helber, Hastert, and Kimura, *North Beach Kaanapali Final Environmental Impact Statement*, "Re: North Beach Kaanapali EIS Preparation Notice and Your Letter dated June 15, 1987," X-29.

255 Helber, Hastert, and Kimura, *North Beach Kaanapali Final Environmental Impact Statement*, "Re: North Beach Kaanapali Draft EIS Your Letter dated October 7, 1987," XII-33.

initiatives to preserve the entire area, says that the first group of intervenors originally held a no-development stance for North Beach, but when they recognized this might not succeed, they began to speak of 2/3rds park space for 1/3 hotels at North Beach. They got less than the opposite. Listening to Draper speak of the fight to preserve North Beach is like hearing a war veteran's account of battle, as he remembers their vigilance to document and speak about the atrocities they saw. The intervenors would feel the personal backlash from the developers for years.

Draper contends that Amfac was altering the site so that the wetlands would become a non-issue. Sand dunes were bulldozed, then filled in with at least 10 feet of sand and debris. Draper also says that the building height was not supposed to exceed two stories, and that the Maui Planning Commission ended up doing whatever its members wanted in response to the various hard fought agreements pushed by community members. Jo Anne Johnson Winer, another intervenor, echoes these sentiments, noting the difficulty of watching what was happening with a growing sense of regret that the area couldn't be saved. A climate of development-without-consensus ran rampant, and the few concessions to the community were simply not good enough.

Due to the toll the long years spent fighting the proposed developments in West Maui took on them individually and collectively, most of these early intervenors were gone when Ka'anapali 2020 rolled around. Many left the dialogue just before the final settlement for Lot 1, and although Randy Draper and other early intervenors like Jo Anne Johnson Winer had held firm to the stance of "no development" at North Beach, what eventually occurred at Keka'a was far from this, as "money got the best of everybody."[256] After meeting religiously and conscientiously for two years to develop the West Maui Community Plan, 80% of what they proposed to ensure slow growth and adequate infrastructure was thrown out the window by the developers and the Maui Planning Commission. Under the guise of caring to hear what the community thought, the developers gathered valuable information from community representatives which they then used to quell the opposition.

Intervenor David Chenowith's testimony before the Maui County Council in 1995 expressed his frustration:

> I, along with other members of this Committee, spent a great deal of time over the past year in taking testimony from our Community, listening to Planning Consultants employed by the County for our use, and following the guidance given to us by the Planning Department. This Committee, after due deliberation, produced a report that gave clear and specific recommendations to be used by the Planning Director for Updating our West Maui Community Plan. This Planning Director had chosen to disregard the very essence of our work. Speaking as a member of the West Maui Citizens Advisor Committee I want to say how disappointed I am in the Plan he has sent to you for your consideration and

256 Randy Draper interview, Napili, Hawai'i, April 10, 2013.

> approval. It provides everything that is needed for continued uncontrolled growth.[257]

The fight to save Keka'a was hard won, then not really won at all, even though some would concede that it did control development at Keka'a. After the no-development contingent had left, Lots 2, 3, and 4 underwent development with constraint. These battles had their own flavor of upset and turmoil. And through this process, the land itself Keka'a, the reefs that front it, and the rivers that flow past—has all been contained, silenced, and incorporated into tourism's master planned agenda.

---

257 David Chenoweth, *Testimony before the Maui County Council Regarding the West Maui Community Plan Update*, September 26, 1995.

Chapter 5: Settlements and the West Maui Preservation Association (WMPA)

Hearings Officer Joel August called the North Beach application 'perhaps the most complex special management area proceeding the county has faced in at least the last 20 years.'[258]

The development of North Beach encompassed all manners of combat and concession—with the results being alternately applauded or dismissed, depending on the perspective and experience of the observer in this process. Some have left the battle worn; others celebrate the accomplishments of scaling back what was initially thought would become another Ka'anapali sized resort in size and girth. But the complicated overall process that went into this subdivision development, played out through the multiple interventions and agreements, lays out a myriad of building and developmental issues on Maui that are difficult to ignore.

---

258 Harry Eager, "N. Beach settlement called 'wonderful,'" *The Maui News*, October 14, 1998, A1.

The Ka'anapali North Beach Subdivision is made up of four lots. Lot 1 consists of the Ka'anapli Ocean Resort, and was approved on December 14, 1998 by the Maui Planning Commission.[259] Lot 2 consists of 11.471 acres and sits adjacent to Lot 1. Lot 3 consists of 10 acres of a public open space area for the Ka'anapali North Beach Subdivision, along with a substantial portion of the drainage system, and will be home to the expansion of the Ka'anapali Ocean Resort Villas, which is not built yet.[260] Lot 4 was developed by Intrawest and is the site of the Honua Kai. The West Maui Preservation Association (WMPA) intervened in Lots 2, 3, and 4. All four Lots that make up the North Beach Subdivision are subject to the Special Management Area Use Permit and the Shoreline Setback Variance, as approved by the Maui Planning Commission on July 19, 1988.[261]

The first Settlement Agreement for North Beach occurred in 1988, when the original North Beach Subdivision application was submitted. These plans called for the development of six hotels, with a total room capacity of 3,200 rooms, configured around two small public parks.[262] The Association of Apartment Owners from the neighboring condominiums at The Mahana

---

259 *Settlement Agreement*, SVO Pacific, Inc. & The West Maui Preservation Association. September 2004, 1.

260 *Settlement Agreement, September 2004*, 10.

261 *Settlement Agreement 2004*, 1.

262 *Findings of Fact, Conclusions of Law, Decision and Order,* Contested Case Hearing: September 22, 1997-October 3, 1997. Nos. 88/SM1-023, 88/SSV-002 and SM1 970006. Maui Planning Commission, Hawai'i, 3.

at Ka'anapali and the Hale Ka'anapali intervened in the Special Management Area Permit (SMA) in May 1988.[263] Traffic congestion was their primary concern and the impetus for the intervention. A Settlement Agreement was then developed between the Ka'anapali North Beach Joint Venture (Amfac Maui and subsidiaries) and the Apartment Owners associations.[264] The Maui Planning Commission granted the SMA and Shoreline Setback Variance on July 19, 1988 to the developers, but this permit came with 19 conditions.[265] The most reviewed condition would become known as Condition Number 7, relating to traffic mitigation measures.

Fast forward almost ten years, when on March 12, 1997, Amfac Maui and Ka'anapali Ownership Resorts, L.P. filed for a SMA to develop the Ka'anapali Ocean Resort (KOR, aka Ka'anapali Vacation Club) on Lot 1 of North Beach.[266] This was the first hotel development proposed, and those who objected were the first group of people to be known in the development documents as the "intervenors," even though they are officially the second group to intervene at North Beach. These intervenors participated in the contested case hearing before Hearing Officer Joel E. August in 1997. A settlement agreement, based partially on August's findings, and also on negotiations between some of the intervenors and the developers, then finalized the

---

263 *Findings of Fact, Conclusions of Law, Decision and Order,* Contested Case Hearing, 5.

264 *Findings of Fact, Conclusions of Law, Decision and Order,* Contested Case Hearing, 6.

265 *Findings of Fact, Conclusions of Law, Decision and Order,* Contested Case Hearing, 6.

266 *Findings of Fact, Conclusions of Law, Decision and Order,* Contested Case Hearing, 7.

Lot 1 development and set the tone for the entire North Beach subdivision.

The Lot 1 settlement in 1998 formally set into motion certain requirements and determined the blueprint for Lots 2, 3, and 4 at North Beach. Issues such as open space jurisdiction, public access, shoreline setbacks, traffic mitigations, and wetland and drainage implications were addressed in this first settlement agreement. And although altered in places, this agreement has served as the guiding document for the future development at Keka'a. But the settlement of Lot 1 was not completed entirely amicably. And even though the settlements that followed seemed to find smoother ground, because the "no development" contingent had all but left the negotiating table, the struggles to preserve some environmental and cultural aspects of Keka'a were still volatile in places. Constant monitoring of and negotiating with developers, and the questioning of WMPA's overall agenda and settlement finances due to the substantial monetary settlements it forged for two community benefit funds, were some of the challenges the next set of intervenors would take up.

The Lot 1 settlement agreement of September 29, 1998 between the Developers—Kaanapali North Beach Joint Venture, AMFAC Property Investment Corp. dba AMFAC Maui, Kaanapali Ownership Resorts, L.P., AMFAC/JMB Hawaii, LLC.—and the Intervenors, Robert Buchanan, David Chenoweth, Elizabeth Chenoweth, Randy Draper, James Johnson, and Joanne Johnson

Winer [267] —led to the approval of the Lot 1 SMA Permit by the Maui Planning Commission for the development of fifty-five one bedroom units and two hundred twenty five two bedroom "lock-off" units (a lock-off unit is a single condominium unit which may be used by the owner as two separate dwelling units).[268]

But half of the intervenors—Randy Draper, James Johnson, and Jo Anne Johnson Winer—actually left the negotiation table just before the settlement was finalized, and so their names were not on the agreement. In fact, it was on September 29, 1998 that Jo Anne and James Johnson formally withdrew their names as intervenors in the case.[269] Differences over what the settlement should contain, and conflicts with their attorney Isaac Hall, resulted in their early exit from the litigation.[270] This was obviously not acknowledged in the settlement agreement itself, which stated that it was in the "spirit of aloha [they] have reached a consensus to resolve the Developers and the Intervenors' concerns."[271] Maybe the Aloha was reserved for the three intervenors who remained.

---

267 *Settlement Agreement,* relating to Kaanapali North Beach, Docket Nos. SM 970006, 88/SM1-023 and 88/SSV-002, Maui Planning Commission, State of Hawaii, September 24, 1998.

268 *Settlement Agreement*, SVO Pacific Inc. and West Maui Preservation Association, October 24, 2007, 2.

269 *Withdrawal of Intervenors JoAnne Johnson Winer and James Johnson; Certificate of Service,* Contested Case Hearings September 22, 1997-October 3, 1997, Maui Planning Commission, September 29, 1998.

270 Statement based on interviews with two of the three intervenors who left litigation.

271 *Settlement Agreement,* September 24, 1998, 2.

The Settlement Agreement for Lot 1 was signed on September 1998; the contested case hearings had finished almost a year prior, on October 1997. These findings led to significant changes incorporated into the Settlement Agreement. According to its opening,

> The Developers and Intervenors have met and discussed their viewpoints on all significant issues, and in the spirit of aloha have reached a consensus to resolve the Developers and the Intervenors' concerns and desire to enter into this agreement.[272]

The significant changes were noted in the Stipulation to Proposed Findings of Fact, Conclusions of Law, Decision and Order. The language regarding open space was radically amended. Its size and location went from the 38.8 acres that Joel E. August had recommended for Lot 4 in the Contested Case Hearing, to a 10-acre parcel on Lot 3. The documents record this smooth transition. To begin with, the County Option to Purchase the 38.8 acres in 1997 emphasized that setting aside a third of the acreage for open space would help resolve most, if not all, of the concerns voiced by the community and the intervenors:

> The County recognizes and agrees that exercising the Option to Purchase will result in a major change in the proposed development, removing one-third of the North Beach Property completely from private development, with a corresponding reduction in density, therefore the widening of Honoapiilani

272 *Settlement Agreement*, September 24, 1998, 2.

Highway from two lanes to four lanes from the Kaanapali Parkway intersection to the Lower Honoapiilani Road intersection is an appropriate traffic mitigation measure that fully complies with the purpose and intent of Condition 7 of the Master SMA for the development of KOR of the North Beach Subdivision.[273]

The contested case hearing reinforced the same idea:

On or about September 22, 1997, the County of Maui entered into an agreement with the owners and developers of the North Beach Subdivision to purchase 33.8 acres at the northern end of the 98-acre subdivision for the sum of $15,000,000 (sic). The parcel to be purchased, known as Lot 4 of the subdivision, would be dedicated for park purposes and, when combined with the previously committed park site at the north end, would create a public beachfront park of approximately 39 acres.

Aside from the public benefit to be derived from the creation of a large beachfront park between Kaanapali and Honokowai, use of Lot 4 as a park would have the effect of reducing the proposed buildout of the subdivision from 3,200 units to 1,950 units. Thus the density of North Beach would be less severe and the corresponding impact upon West Maui's physical and public service infrastructure would be reduced.[274]

One year later, this was noted and written in bold in the

---

273 *Option to Purchase,* Amfac Property Investment Corp. to County of Maui, September 19, 1997, 7.

274 *Findings of Fact, Conclusions of Law, Decision and Order,* Contested Case Hearing, 28.

Stipulation to Proposed Findings of Fact, Conclusions of Law, Decision and Order:

> **Construction of a public beach park of not less than 38.8 acres at North Beach must be commenced prior to a certificate of occupancy being issued for phase II of the Kaanapali Ocean Resort.**
>
> **This language should be replaced by the following:**
>
> **A Public Open Space/Recreation Area, ten acres in size, as agreed upon by the parties, shall be open and available, in perpetuity, for public uses for open space, parking and passive recreational uses as well as for certain Native Hawaiian traditional and customary uses, based upon the terms of the Settlement Agreement and the "Declaration of Perpetual Rights and Uses and Perpetual Restrictions" agreed to by the Applicant.**[275]

The Settlement Agreement therefore drastically changed what Joel E. August had deemed necessary—most notably, the amount of acreage set aside for open space. In 1998, Joel E. August had remarked, "It made me feel good that both of them (Amfac and the intervenors) were extremely unhappy with my decision."[276] But when asked recently about the change in open

---

275 *Stipulation to Proposed Findings of Fact, Conclusions of Law, Decision and Order*, Maui Planning Commission, Docket Nos.: 88/SM1-023, 88/SSV-002, and SM 970006, Deptember 30, 1998, 10-11.

276 Harry Eager, "N. Beach settlement called 'wonderful,'" A1.

space acreage from 38.8 acres to 10 acres, August was unaware and surprised that the park requirements had changed.[277] Also, the 10 acres in Lot 3 adjoin the land set aside for drainage for the entire area. Some still contend that putting a park in a space that occasionally floods does little to serve the public good.

The shoreline setback area for the subdivision was set at 150 feet in the Stipulation to Proposed Findings of Fact, Conclusions of Law, Decision and Order. This area

> **shall be open and available, in perpetuity, to members of the public for open space, parking and passive recreational uses as well as for certain Native Hawaiian traditional and customary uses based upon the terms of the Settlement Agreement and the Declaration of Perpetual Rights and Uses and Perpetual Restrictions applicable to the Shoreline Setback Area agreed to by the Applicant.**[278]

No commercial activity, or large structures other than barbeque pits and picnic tables, would be allowed in the open space/recreation and setback areas. The setback areas were to be landscaped "or left in a relatively natural state."[279] And even though the open space acreage was smaller, the total number of units was to "never exceed 1,950."[280] So 28.8 acres were reallocated for development—a substantial amount for a

277 Phone interview with Joel E. August, September 2013.

278 *Stipulation to Proposed Findings of Fact, Conclusions of Law, Decision and Order*, 11.

279 *Settlement Agreement, September 24, 1998*, 8.

280 *Settlement Agreement, September 24, 1998*, 8.

95-acre subdivision—but a 10 acre open-space area and a 150 foot shoreline setback area are set aside for the public and for "present and future native Hawaiians for certain native Hawaiian traditional and customary uses, as follows: fishing, diving, hoʻokupu ceremonies (ritual group prayers on the shoreline), and gathering."[281]

But finding ways to alleviate what could become a traffic nightmare was the primary concern in these early documents, and through the years. Various traffic mitigation measures were agreed to, but not necessarily welcomed, by the larger community. Some of the language pertaining to traffic congestion was also altered in the Stipulation to Proposed Findings of Fact, Conclusions of Law, Decision and Order. David Blane, then Director of Planning, originally testified unfavorably towards building North Beach without the Lahaina Bypass Highway in place and functioning as a commuter passage way. What he originally wrote to the Planning Commission, already shared in the previous chapter, was:

> Please consider this letter as an addendum to the Director's Report dated December 10, 1996, regarding Amfac Maui's request to have the widening of Honoapiilani Highway considered as a mitigative measure for the proposed construction of their Kaanapali Vacation Club. At this time, I would like to inform the Commissioners that the Planning Department does not feel that

281 *Settlement Agreement, September 24, 1998*, 7-8.

the proposal constitutes adequate mitigative measures and, therefore, does not support this request.

After reviewing the lengthy history of this issue it is clear to me that the Lahaina Bypass was always considered a necessity before any North Beach hotels could be built. The thread of this assumption winds through all the subsequent approvals including the West Maui Community Plan that was adopted by the Council on February 27, 1996. Although detailed traffic calculations may show that the proposed widening of this section of Honoapiilani Highway may address the short-term traffic impacts of this hotel, the Department must evaluate this proposal over the long term.[282]

Blane's later testimony confirmed this early letter:

At the contested case hearing on the Kaanapali Ocean Resort SMA application, David W. Blane testified in his capacity as Planning Director that the widening of Honoapiilani Highway between Kaanapali Parkway and Honokowai Stream would satisfy the "other mitigating measures" requirement of Condition 7 if the entire North Beach Subdivision were limited to a total buildout of only 1950 units [and if the County were able to develop the 33.8 acres as a public park]. Absent these conditions, Mr. Blane indicated he would still advocate the conclusions stated in his letter of December 6, 1996.[283]

Combining the two ideas above, a general statement not

282 *Contested Case Hearing,* 10.

283 *Stipulation to Proposed Findings of Fact, Conclusions of Law, Decision and Order,* 4.

explicitly attached to Blane's testimony appeared as Condition 7 in the Settlement Agreement:

> Satisfaction of Condition 7
>
> The four lane road widening improvements currently proposed for Honoapiilani Highway (between Kaanapali Parkway and the Honokowai Stream) suffices to satisfy the additional traffic demands created by KOR and the Public Open Space/ Recreation Area, and thus, satisfy Condition 7 with respect to the KOR project and the Public Open Space/Recreation Area. The provisions of this paragraph are without prejudice to the rights of the parties to submit their own facts, opinions and/or legal arguments with respect to whether the four lane road widening improvements currently proposed for the Honoapiilani Highway will or will not satisfy the additional traffic demands created by any additional development after KOR within the Subdivision. In the event that said highway improvements are delayed or deferred by the initiation of a lawsuit by any person or entity other than Developers, then Developers shall have the right to void this Agreement upon surrendering of the SMA permit for KOR.[284]

In essence, this settlement applied Condition 7 to Lot 1, not to the entire development, as was always the intention in the prior proceedings regarding the development of North Beach as a whole.

In addition to these dramatic changes from the contested

284 *Settlement Agreement*, 19.

case hearing to the settlement, one big concession conjured up a well thought out drainage system known as the *Master Drainage Plan*.[285] This plan insured that runoff and wetland waters would not drain directly into near shore waters, and that storage basins and off-site drainage areas would be created by the developers. As *The Maui News* reported:

> A new drainage plan that will not allow storm water to be directly discharged into the nearshore water. Amfac also will provide retention areas mauka of the project to retain storm runoff. The goal is to return the runoff storage capacity of the area to its 1988 condition.[286]

A water quality management program would also ensure Best Management Practices for pesticides and irrigation, and include other ways to mitigate pollution and water quality control.[287] A civil engineer and marine biologist would be employed to monitor the effectiveness of the Master Drainage Plan. A Unilateral Declaration of Restrictions was signed to insure that the North Beach Unit Count and Drainage requirements would "run with the land in perpetuity."[288]

The one big question that fueled all of the intervenors',

---

285 *Settlement Agreement,* 15.

286 "Agreement reached on North Beach time-share project," *The Maui News*, October 6, 1998, A2.

287 *Settlement Agreement,* 13.

288 *Unilateral Declaration of Restrictions, North Beach Unit Count and Drainage.* Amfac Property Investment Corp. (APIC), October 7, 1998.

and eventually for the developers', was whether the overall construction of the project would have any adverse consequences for the area. At first, the official answer was yes:

> The Commission finds there is sufficient evidence in the record to conclude that the Kaanapali Ocean Resort development, combined with the future plans for North Beach, will have a substantial adverse environmental or ecological impact upon the subject coastal zone.[289]

But this statement was revised to read that the development would not cause adverse consequences if some conditions, hammered out between the developers and three of the first intervenors, were observed. The SMA was granted based on these "spirit of Aloha" conclusions, to be monitored by an Advisory Group made up of nine West Maui residents for five years from the date of implementation. The intervenors appointed four members; the developers and Amfac appointed the other five.[290]

As the *Lahaina News* reported, "Interveners David and Elizabeth Chenoweth and Robert Buchanan do not oppose the time share if the terms of the agreement are met. Interveners Randy Draper and James and JoAnne Johnson Winer did not sign the agreement."[291] The ones who did not sign off left the litigation after exhausting their resources on expensive legal

---

289 *Contested Case Hearing,* 46.

290 *Settlement Agreement,* 18.

291 Mark Veith, "Beach access, cap on units part of pact on North Beach resort," *Lahaina News*. Vol. 19, No. 41.

fees, and over differences with their lawyer about how their complaints were being relayed to the opposition. They felt their concerns were not being addressed or met.[292] The ones who stayed on were presumably satisfied with the results. Kumu Hula Roselle Bailey and Buck Buchanan were among those at the dedication of the "Keka'a Open Space Recreational Area" in 2002, a ceremony celebrating the 10 acres of open space, and the shoreline and parking access.[293]

For his part, in an interview with *The Maui News*, Isaac Hall said:

> 'We're very excited about this agreement. We're happy we've been able to work cooperatively with Amfac and (its president) Gary Gottke and the attorneys.' Hall said the terms break new ground. He said it is the first contested case agreement that 'makes a real effort to comply with PASH [Public Access Shoreline Hawai'i] and Native Hawaiian traditional and customary rights.'[294] Hall told the commission the settlement agreement may seem to disagree with some of August's findings but that really it should be viewed as a novel way of arranging mitigation.[295]

But even with the settlement agreement, development

---

292 Based on interviews with Jo Anne Johnson Winer and Randy Draper.

293 "Kekaa Open Space Recreational Area dedicated," *The Maui News,* January 16, 2002, 1.

294 Harry Eager, "Agreement reached on N. Beach: Faction opposing time-share project 'happy' with terms," *The Maui News*, October 6, 1998, A2.

295 Harry Eager, "Planning Commission hears terms and reasons for pact," *The Maui News,* October 14, 1998, A2.

of Lot 1 was not necessarily a sure thing in 1998. The Maui Planning Commission first voted against the SMA on October 19, 1998, based on the "D" ranking the state gave the widening of the highway, because this mitigative measure would do little to help with increased traffic flow. "Then the hard negotiating began,"[296] and the Commission passed the SMA soon after. Then in came the next group of intervenors who dealt with Lots 2, 3, and 4 at North Beach.

Spearheaded by WMPA (West Maui Preservation Association), more interventions and settlements followed. WMPA began in 2004 as a nonprofit organization "for the purpose of preserving, protecting and restoring the natural and cultural environment of West Maui, including land conservation and educational activities related thereto."[297] More specifically, the WMPA mission included

> Improvement projects, including land acquisition, for betterment, preservation, maintenance, and protection of ocean, reef, marine life, shoreline, dunes, parks, open spaces, roadways, parking facilities, and other areas of Ka'anapali North Beach and West Maui, thereby enhancing the natural beauty and public enjoyment of the West Maui region.[298]

Over the next few years, WMPA negotiated funding from

---

296 Harry Eager, "North Beach SMA rejected—but not quite finally," *The Maui News*, October 20, 1998, A3.

297 http://www.savewestmaui.com/mission.htm, cited 12/28/2012.

298 http://www.savewestmaui.com/mission.htm, cited 12/28/2012.

the developers for the continued preservation of North Beach, while making sure that both new and already agreed upon development restrictions were recognized and followed.

The developers of Lot 2 filed for a Shoreline Management Area Permit for the Westin Ka'anapali Ocean Resort Villas Expansion, a time-share resort with 258 two-bedroom "lock off" units, with the Maui Planning Commission on November 21, 2003, followed by a supplemental report on July 6, 2004.[299] Three months after its formation in June 2004, the non-profit WMPA filed a Petition to Intervene in the Shoreline Management Area application of Starwood Hotels Resorts Worldwide Inc. at North Beach on August 6, 2004. It was deferred until September 14, 2004, so that the parties could come together and reach an agreement. They did, and the Maui Planning Commission approved the SMA on October 8, 2004.[300]

Lot 2, TMK 4-4-14:004, is on 11.471 acres of land. As submitted, its expansion would have adversely affected the area through drainage runoff of dirt into the ocean, the loss or damage of the sand dunes, and increased traffic flow from Honoapi'ilani Highway for the entire area. This development was also threatening to become a nuisance once again for the owners of the Mahana condominiums located just north of North Beach. WMPA's president, Sharyn Matin, had a Mahana

299 *Settlement Agreement Lot 3*, SVO Pacific, Inc., and the West Maui Preservation Association, October 24, 2007, 3.

300 *Settlement Agreement Lot 3*, 3.

condominium, and the petition reflected a two fold argument: "The proposed development, as currently planned, will adversely affect Ms. Matin and other supporters of the WMPA, because it will diminish their use and enjoyment of their properties and cause economic harm to them. It will have adverse impacts on protected resources within the CZMA (Coastal Zone Management Area)."[301] Unlike the early Lot 1 Petition to Intervene, this one did not seek to halt the development outright: "One of the questions this time will be: How big is the resort?"[302]

The Petition to Intervene was withdrawn by WMPA after negotiations with Starwood proved successful, and in September 2004, SVO Pacific, Inc. and WMPA signed a Settlement Agreement for Lot 2. The developer concessions were substantial, including a large donation and yearly payments to establish and maintain a non-profit known in brief as the "Benefit Fund." A Lot 4 Petition to Intervene was filed at the same time, and a letter sent to the owners at the Mahana in February 2005 listed some concessions engineered by WMPA for both Lots 2 and 4:

[Besides no piledriving anywhere in current North Beach Projects], Additional benefits were gained in our two negotiated settlements. A few of those are:

- Complete removal of 80-feet of the building closest to Mahana and the shoreline.

301 "Association Challenging North Beach Project," 1.

302 Harry Eager, "Kaanapali Ocean Villas time share deferred for more talks," *The Maui News*, August 25, 2004.

- Installation of a beach walkway from Mahana to the public park at the south end of the cane field (Kahekili Park).
- Elevated walkway bridges over the dunes connecting the beach to that walkway.
- Installation of a new fence on IW's property to protect Mahana's Monkeypod trees.
- Addition of a 20-ft grass firelane between Mahana and IW's nearest building extending to the kiawe grove at shoreline. There was previously NO firelane on IW's project.
- Vastly improved drainage systems at both resorts, and on the hills across the highway.
- Sewage to be sent to Napili, not to the plant across the street from Mahana, with backflow valves requested for Mahana and the other 3 condos on that line.
- Height reductions to both of IW's buildings, particularly at IW's wing closest to Mahana.
- The spire with flag, and the neon light decoration atop those two buildings has been removed.
- Community Benefit Trust Fund to assist in WMPA's current proposed projects of Honokowai Channel redesign to stop red dirt runoff from closing use of the ocean at North Beach, and repaving Honokowai Road in front of Ka'anapali Shores Resort.
- Acquisition of easement and relocation of the 3-Resort location sign after installation of a dedicated right turn lane along Honokowai Road from Mahana's road to the Highway.
- Enlargement of the new North Park next to Mahana, with addition of grass areas at the shoreline and side, and with attractive landscaping added throughout the new park.

- Side setback increase, moving IW's nearest building farther south from Mahana.
- Placement of a large thicket of 20-ft tall trees in the new North Park to minimize wind.[303]

In addition, Intrawest agreed to provide cash contributions: $2.75M in traffic impact fees, $650,000 in increments to a trust for projects that will benefit West Maui that could include roads, hospitals or schools, and $100,000 to WMPA, also for preservation efforts.[304]

Donations of $500,000 were also made to Lahaianaluna High School Foundation, and $1.4 million to the West Maui Resource Center for its affordable housing requirement. In return for these concessions, WMPA withdrew its Petition(s) to Intervene on Lots 2 & 4, and Intrawest built a 700 unit condo hotel at North Beach on Lot 4, with prices that ranged from $500,000 to $2 Million.[305] Attorney Hall was paid $24,512 in legal fees by the developers, along with the other monetary concessions.[306]

---

303 Letter to Mahana Owners—February 11th, 2005. http://www.savewestmaui.com/letter_050211.htm, cited January 3, 2013.

304 Valerie Monson, "Condo Project Ok'd. Intervention Assures Kaanapali Plans won't hurt North Beach Dunes," *The Maui News*, February 25, 2005, 2. http:www.savewestmaui.com/news_mauinews_050225.htm.

305 Valerie Monson, 2.

306 Gwen Ohashi Hiraga, Project Manager, RE: *Special Management Area Use Permit and Step 2 Planned Development Applications for the Proposed Honua Kai Resort, North Beach and Related Improvements*, Report to Maui Planning Commission, March 1, 2007, 4.

Additional concessions from the developer for Lot 2 were:

A Drainage plan that would be discharged into the "trapezoidal basin" located on Lot 3.[307]

A community fund to be called the "North Beach/West Maui Benefit Fund" (the "Benefit Fund") by means of a trust agreement or other appropriate entity or entities, in form and content reasonably acceptable to Petitioner and Developer."

"The Benefit Fund will be expressly and perpetually limited and restricted for use for designated improvement projects, including land acquisitions, improvement of coastal resources, roadway improvements and other appropriate benefits to the North Beach/West Maui area and community, all as determined from time to time by the Board, overseeing use of the Benefit Fund.[308]

The Board for this fund was initially comprised of Sharyn Martin, Charles Fox (attorney), Philip Goosens (founding member of WMPA), Jeffrey Jones (WMPA member), and one representative designated by the developer.[309] The funds could be used to pay attorneys' fees for proceedings only if they are not related to North Beach, and the overall funding occurred only if the developer received final written approval from the Maui Planning Commission for the Lot 2 SMA Permit within 30 days of the agreement.[310] The developer also agreed to

307 *Settlement Agreement,* SVO Pacific, Inc., and The West Maui Preservation Association, September 2004, 2.

308 *Settlement Agreement, September 2004*, 4.

309 *Settlement Agreement 2004,* 4.

310 *Settlement Agreement 2004*, 5.

deposit $425,000 into a joint escrow account for the Benefit Fund once created, but only after "the final, non-appealable approval and issuance by the County of Maui of building permits for the contemplated Westin Ka'anapali Ocean Resort Villas Expansion."[311] Like the other agreements, this deal hinged on official approval: "Termination of Agreement. If the Lot 2 SMA Permit is not approved by the Maui Planning Commission, then and in such event, this Agreement shall be automatically rendered null and void."[312]

The developer actually paid $1,000,000 in to the Benefit Fund, dependent upon approval of the Lot 2 SMA.[313] An annual contribution of $10 for each time-share sold for that year also was paid,[314] with the maximum dollar amount of the fund not exceeding two million.[315] Dune management, water quality, and traffic mitigation were also negotiated in the SMA. The North Beach West Maui Benefit Fund is the non-profit formed from this settlement—with the Ka'anapali Development Corporation the successor of Amfac, as was the North Beach Mauka/Makai Advisory Group—while the benefit fund is separate from WMPA, Sharyn Martin serves as president of both non-profits.

On March 26, 2006, an amendment to the SMA was approved for the installation of a parking structure and a second emergency

---

311 *Settlement Agreement 2004,* 5.

312 *Settlement Agreement 2004,* 13.

313 *Settlement Agreement 2004,* 6.

314 *Settlement Agreement 2004,* 6.

315 *Settlement Agreement 2004,* 7.

access lane. The water table was higher than expected and so raising the parking structure was required, with no change in the number of parking stalls. The original SMA granted on October 8, 2004 was therefore modified to accommodate a parking deck two feet lower near Honoapi'ilani Highway, and seven feet higher at the rear, and for the installation of security gates for Lot 2 and Lot 3. On September 30, 2006, the Westin Ka'anapali Ocean Resort began building the 258 unit time-share in six phases over a five year time period. The developers also contributed 1.5 million dollars for the Keawe Street extensions.

A Grant of Easement also went into effect on October 1, 2004. This allowed two additional storm water retention and storage basins to be added to the two already present. Since "The Existing Retention Basins are an integral part of the off-site storm water drainage system for the Ka'anapali North beach Subdivision, as set forth in the Drainage Master Plan and in accordance with the 2001 Drainage Declaration,"[316] the storm water storage runoff with the four Retention Basins was estimated to be 1,130,000 cubic feet, "of which amount 658,000 cubic feet shall be deemed exclusively allocated for the benefit of Lot 1 and Lot 2."[317] As the documents keep showing, in a district thought to be extremely dry, Keka'a seems to be the exception to the rule. Because the

---

316 *Grant of Easement and Agreement Regarding Allocation of Retention Capacity, North Beach—Mauka Retention Basins*, Land Court TMK No. (2)4-4-2:039 (POR), October 20, 2004, 2.

317 *Grant of Easement and Agreement Regarding Allocation of Retention Capacity, North Beach—Mauka Retention Basins*, 2.

Northern region of the Lahaina District is wetter than the southern, altering the landscape to accomodate the tourist gaze was necessary and extensive. Simply put, you can't build hotels on swamp land—see the creation and manipulation of the landscape of Waikīkī. Drain and fill, or retain, divert or simply let dry out, is how the Ka'anapali resort experience was extended to North Beach.

The Lot 4 Settlement Agreement was also in this mix, and some of the related concessions are listed above. This February 2, 2005 settlement between the Maui Beach Resort Limited Partnership and The West Maui Preservation Association[318] dealt with the Honua Kai development, wetland and drainage issues, and more traffic mitigation measures. The wetland was finally recognized by the Army Corps of Engineers after a survey conducted on August 6, 2004.[319] The agreement mandated that the developer could either choose the avoidance option, or could enhance the wetland with vegetative clearing, replanting, and silt removal.[320] Off-site drainage initiatives, along with water quality monitoring for Lot 4, were also clarified and plans incorporated for both.

The Dune Management Program is another initiative that came out of this settlement. A licensed coastal engineer was hired with the go-ahead from the developer and WMPA. The elevated

318 *Settlement Agreement*, Maui Beach Resort Limited Partnership and The West Maui Preservation Association, Inc. February 2, 2005.

319 *Settlement Agreement,* February 2, 2005, 1.

320 *Settlement Agreement,* February 2, 2005, 2.

walkway, the eradication of Kiawe trees, and the maintenance of the sand dunes were a few responsibilities of this program. The 150-foot setback was recognized, and an elevated walkway, instituted to control lounge chairs from rolling over the dunes, was introduced as a new initiative. Finally, a section of Lot 4 named "North Park" would provide public access, fences, and gates fronting the neighboring Mahana.

In response to the traffic concerns mentioned in Matin's letter to the owners at The Mahana, "The Developer will provide a contribution of $2,5000,000 for traffic improvements as discussed with the County of Maui."[321] These would include roadwork on Honoapi'ilani Highway and Halawai Drive, signage, and traffic light synchronization in Lahaina. The study and execution of that ever-present entity, the Lahaina Bypass Highway, was also funded.

Finally, the developer would contribute to a community benefit fund from the Lot 4 Settlement. Known as the Honua Kai West Maui Community Trust (HKWMCF), this tax exempt non-profit organization would

> Be used only for projects and goals such as land acquisitions, improvement of coastal resources, recreational improvements, roadway improvements, scholarships, Native Hawaiian cultural purposes and other appropriate benefits to the North Beach/ West Maui area and community.[322]

---

321 *Settlement Agreement,* February 2, 2005, 6.

322 *Settlement Agreement,* February 2, 2005, 7.

The HKWMCF Board of Directors has five members—three appointed by both the developer and WMPA, one appointed by the developer, and one appointed by WMPA. The fund initially received $400,000 held in escrow until the 501(c)(3) tax exemption status was established. The on-going funding mechanism for this fund is a .25% transfer fee paid to on sale of all residential units.[323] The fund also received an annual lump sum of $50,000 from the developer for five years, for a total of $250,000.[324]

In March 2007, Munekiyo, Hiraga, and Hirano submitted an informational report on the Honua Kai Resort to the Maui Planning Commission, detailing the firm's dispersal of funds as representative of the developer to WMPA and Maui County. This report fulfilled Condition No. 32 for the SMA approval of Lot 4: "That an annual report shall be filed with the Maui Planning Commission on the disbursement of the funds in the Settlement Agreements for their information."[325] This report made this settlement agreement public, and simply recorded the dates when the funds were transferred to WMPA, the County, and to the Lahainaluna High School Foundation. But then the Maui Planning Commission began questioning the WMPA about the use of the funds. The February 28, 2006 minutes of the

323 *Settlement Agreement*, February 2, 2005, 8.

324 *Settlement Agreement*, February 2, 2005, 8.

325 Munekiyo & Hiraga, Inc., *Special Management Area Use Permit and Step 2 Planned Development Applications for the Proposed Honua Kai Resort, North Beach Park and Related Improvements*. March 7, 2007, 1.

MPC indicate that Mr. Sewall of Intrawest and Sharon Matin of WMPA, were questioned. Gwen Hiraga of Intrawest provided an update of the settlement between Intrawest and WMPA; the Commission had questions about the $1.53 million contribution for traffic mitigation, and the $400,000 for the Benefit Fund, noting that almost a year after the settlement, it still had not been established. Steve Sewall of Intrawest explained and the Commissioners and Matin replied:

> Mr. Sewall: The guidelines that were setup in the settlement agreement is that we would fund a nonprofit association that would be made up of five members from the community [that] would actually have the authority to make the decisions on how that money got spent. We at this point have our $400,000 sitting in Title Guaranty in accordance with the other clause we'll have to put another $50,000 on the anniversary date which would be this month. The nonprofit as far as the structure of the nonprofit and how it's registered, in our settlement agreement was actually made the responsibility of WMPA to actually set that up and register it accordingly.
>
> Mr. Casumpang: With regards to that $400,000 sitting in escrow and doing nothing.
>
> Ms. Matin: Yes.
>
> Mr. Casumpang: Please don't get me wrong, that your organization get that money, it's we the commission even get hard time to impose impact fees, but I'm glad that you're able to get that monies. But knowing that it's sitting there doing nothing, and that's what my concern is.
>
> Ms. Matin: Yes, and that's my concern as well. The problem is, I

did not know until receiving Gwen's letter that—where the funds had been placed. All that we were told previously to Gwen's letter was that it was in a trust or an escrow and there was later a verbal that oh, it was in escrow. I had no idea who or where held it. I have, it's presently under a single signature as I understand it of Intrawest to make the deposit. Under the settlement agreement it should be under double escrow, we can then put WMPA's W-9 on file with the escrow company so that interest can be collected and do an escrow agreement which will say the escrow remains open until the nonprofit is formed then it transfers over, in the meantime it collects interest. WMPA would be paying the taxes on that interest in order to have it bear interest until it is formed.

Mr. Hedani: Okay. The other question that I had was the $100,000 that was set aside for the association, what does that go to?

Ms. Matin: The $100,000 was a contribution to WMPA. We are using that for obtaining, maintaining our 501 and for setting up the nonprofit that will be administering the community benefit.

Mr. Hedani: But it doesn't cost a $100,000 to set up 501©(3).

Ms. Matin: No, it doesn't but that is to maintain it throughout the life. Okay. And once we get the other one set up we already have community benefit projects started which the community members of the new nonprofit may wish to take on or join in or they may wish to go a different direction.

Ms. Moikeha: I don't consider this $100,000 to keep your organization running under a nonprofit status with the Federal Government accomplishing that. So do you see the conflict that this commission has and why we are really—

Ms. Matin: I understand that.[326]

---

326 *Maui Planning Commission Minutes—February 28, 2006*, 33-63, 36 & 54.

This line of questioning continued on this particular day. The questioning also continued in the March 13, 2007 Maui Planning Commission minutes. Lance Collins, the attorney that took Isaac Hall's place as the attorney for WMPA, responded to the questioning:

> Mr. Lance Collins: Hi, Lance Collins, I'm the attorney for WMPA. I think that—yeah, no, she—Judge Matin is the president of the non profit. I'm the attorney for it. September 14th, right I understand, September 14th of last year we notified you folks that I became the attorney of record.
>
> I think that maybe what's happening here is the entity was incorporated and it has been formed and the next step once that occurs is to get the double signature account on the escrow. So I think, both of your questions are being answered. It has been formed, it was incorporated, excuse me, over it was two years ago?
>
> Ms. Matin: The articles—
>
> Mr. Collins: Yeah, articles.
>
> Ms. Matin: —have not been filed for the lack of the escrow funds.
>
> Mr. Collins: Right for the lack of the escrow funding but they have been finished. Attorney Welch has finished this. We have constantly been asking Intra West, you know, it can't be done only by WMPA because it's a collaborative effort by both Intra West and WMPA and you're essentially raising your voice to her. And all she's saying is is that there's a procedure that requires their participation and they have not been responding to that, and so I think it's a little unfair to be attacking her when at this point—if there's supposed to be five people and they have to concur with

all those five people and they're not communicating about that, you cannot blame WMPA solely for all of this.[327]

The questioning of why the Benefit Fund was not set up, the overall integrity of WMPA, and confusion about the settlement agreement itself between WMPA and Intrawest continued to fuel the questioning in these minutes. For their part, WMPA continued to state that they were in fact waiting for the participation of Intrawest.

On April 10, 2007, Wayne Hedani, Chairman of the Planning Commission, sent Sharyn Matin a letter asking for an accounting of $125,000 that WMPA received from Maui Beach Resort Limited Partnership. Lance Collins responded to the letter, in essence asking the Commission to be clear about what it was asking for:

> While your letter requests an accounting of $125,000 given to West Maui Preservation Association by Intrawest, numbers ranging from 100,000 to $400,000 to $500,000 were used by different commissioners during that portion of the meeting.
> To clarify the position of the Maui Planning Commission, I am requesting, in behalf of the West Maui Preservation Association, that the Commission, by the required majority vote, articulate

327 *Maui Planning Commission Minutes—March 13, 2007,* p. 92-118, 102.

what accounting it's seeking and if it has jurisdiction to compel such an accounting, identifying such authority.[328]

In the Maui Planning Commission regular meeting that followed on May 8, 2007, the arguments did another round, the bottom line was that a private settlement agreement is private between the parties and the Maui Planning Commission has no jurisdiction over that agreement. Lance Collins contends that the Commissioners are confusing the matters, as some were present during the time of the settlements, and some are newer members to the commission. Some seem to be purposely creating confusion to diminish the good work that WMPA has done in West Maui and cast doubt on the process of intervention in general.

At the 2007 meeting, the Commissioners only wanted to know about the funding to WMPA and refused to allow Matin to speak about inadequacies with the developer's other funding obligations. The Office of Information Practices ruled in 2007 that the commissioners violated the Sunshine Law by not allowing Matin to give testimony but only answer their specific questions.[329] In response to this action, Anthony Pignataro wrote that

---

328 Collins to Hedani, *Maui Planning Commission Requesting an Account of the Disbursement of Funds to West Maui Preservation Association from Maui Beach LP,* April 17, 2007.

329 See Opinion, Office of the Lieutenant Governor as Appendix A.

> It's rare to see a county official—especially one making $92,300 a year—screw up so badly in public that the state Office of Information Practices (OIP) gets to slap him or her across the wrist. Suyama's little act of impropriety occurred way back on March 13 of this year, during a Maui Planning Commission hearing. According to the five-page OIP opinion issued yesterday, during the hearing Suyama "violated the Sunshine Law" by restricting the testimony of Sharyn Matin, a private citizen and president of the West Maui Preservation Association (WMPA).[330]

Although not required to make public, the uses of the funds that went to WMPA have been disclosed annually by the filing of annual information tax returns available on the internet. WMPA has not been back to testify before the Maui Planning Commission since 2007.

But, current Maui Planning Commission testimony reflects that even though WMPA is not present at the meetings, the questioning has not abated:

> Mr. Prutch: There used to be two intervenors. It was Charlie Fox and WMPA. Charlie Fox funds have all been paid in full I think two years ago. We're pau with Charlie Fox, but the WMPA money is still being paid. So far what I have calculated is the amount to be disbursed to WMPA was about 2.1 million. The amount disbursed so far is about 1.2, so there's still about $887,000 remains and from last year's report to this year's report, I saw

330 Anthony Pignataro, *Maui Time Weekly,* July 5, 2007.

that it was about $192,000 was paid for the Mill Street Extension Traffic Study.[331]

Mr. Sewall: The 25 percent that, you know, came up previously on resales in the project, we're not specifically doing the resales. We still have units that we're selling ourselves, but we're not you know targeting any of the resales on it. And it only does come off of resale units. It doesn't come off any of the first-time around sold units. So but I know those funds are still being distributed to WMPA, but I've got no knowledge of, you know, any use of those funds to date. So I don't know what they've been spending the money on, but it was more than just that 25 percent. We gave them a fairly significant amount of start up cash or whatever you wanna call it at the time that the settlement was done as well.[332]

Collins says, "WMPA has and will not be receiving any further moneys from the Developer or the agreement and hasn't since 2005. The resales go directly to and fund the Lot 4 community fund non-profit. WMPA has nothing to do with that."[333] Collins also contends that the new Deputy Planning Director, Michelle McLean, called WMPA to come to the meeting in 2012, but after reviewing the on-line tax reports, she was satisfied with the information provided.

Besides these issues, the Lot 4 Honua Kai development encountered other challenges along the way, the primary one

---

331 *Maui Planning Commision Minutes—May 28, 2013*, p. 38-48, 38.

332 *Maui Planning Commision Minutes—May 28, 2013*, 45-46.

333 Lance Collins, email correspondense, September 15, 2013. Also, see Collins letter to MPC as Appendix B.

being the building of Duke's restaurant (TS Restaurants) on the premises. On November 20, 2007, Intrawest sent Colleen Suyama, then Deputy Planning Director and now Senior Associate at Munekiyo and Hiraga, Inc., the planning and consulting firm for Amfac Maui, wrote a letter regarding the need for a change to the SMA that would permit a large scale restaurant on the premises. Intrawest was trying to convince the Planning Commission that increasing the square footage by 3,400, and providing a three meal a day restaurant, met the intent of the snack bar type food structure agreed upon in the original SMA.[334]

Intrawest scheduled a request with the Maui County Urban Review Board. Attorney Collins filed a Petition for Writ of Quo Warranto against Suyama for shirking her responsibility by referring the matter to the Urban Review Board, instead of taking the matter up with the Commission.[335]

> Petitioner appears to be claiming that Respondent Colleen Suyama, Deputy Director of the Department of Planning for the county, illegally delegated some decision-making authority to the Planning Department or Planning Commission.[336]

The matter was denied. The petition was referred to

---

334 Munekiyo & Suyama to Deputy Director Colleen Suyama, *Honua Kai Resort—Proposed Restaurant Revisions,* November 21, 2007.

335 *Petition for Writ of Quo Warranto,* Second Circuit Court, State of Hawaii, January 10, 2008.

336 *Findings and Order Denying Petition for Writ of Quo Warranto,* Second Circuit Court, Sate of Hawaii, January 10, 2008.

the courtroom of state Circuit Court Judge Joel E. August who ultimately denied the request with a written opinion. Nevertheless, it did produce a settlement between the developer and WMPA. Duke's was built through direct negotiations between WMPA and TS Restaurants in three separate meetings. One substantial change to the plans was that a planned underground tunnel for transporting food was stopped because the land was too saturated to support and ensure the safety of such a structure. In a separate incident, in 2010 "A dozen purchasers at Honua Kai have sued to overturn their sales contracts and receive refunds for payments they made."[337]

With these challenges came other transitions at the Honua Kai resort. One was the opening of a 5-acre park negotiated by WMPA and the developers: "The passive park is open to the general public and provides beach access at the north end of the subdivision; 106 parking stalls, plus six handicap spaces; a comfort station; picnic tables; and barbecue stations."[338] Also noteworthy is the resort's recycling and sustainability program. Duke's restaurant has an "eco-rubber" roofing material, composed of recycled tires.[339] A *Lahaina News* article also featured the work of the members of the North Beach Advisory Group: Aunty Patty Nishiyama, Henry "Bruno" Ariyoshi, John

337 Harry Eager, "Intrawest's second tower of new Honua Kai slated for 2010," *The Maui News*, February 6, 2009, 1.

338 Louise Rockett, "Honua Kai dedicates new five-acre park," *Lahaina News,* February 11, 2010, 1.

339 Louise Rockett, "Honua Kai dedicates new five-acre park," 2.

Kuia, Buck Buchanan, Star Medeiros and Walter De Los Reyes. Development manager Anthony Plitt remarked:

> We meet monthly and really do give the NBAG work to do. Usually, within a month, it's turned around, and we have our answers from street naming to the park naming; to color selection for the park buildings to choice of barbecues and picnic tables; where the parking stalls should go; what type of grass should we plant; where the trees should go...what are we doing with the wood from the kiawe trees; who can we help and give that to; Donate it to local groups for barbecuing or up at Lahainaluna for wood working class... things like that. They are helping us keep connected. They really do serve the community. I truly believe that they have a huge input to our project and its success.[340]

The final settlement at North Beach was the Lot 3 Settlement Agreement, signed on October 24, 2007, between SVO Pacific, Inc., and WMPA.[341] This agreement solidified the development of "the final phase of [the] Ka'anapali Ocean Resort Villas and Westin Ka'anapali Ocean Resort Villas North."[342] Lot 3 contains 26.7 acres and is recorded as TMK No. (2) 4-4-0014:005 (por).[343] The proposed development was for the construction of 390 one, two, and three bedroom units that would not intrude into the

---

340 Louise Rockett, "Honua Kai dedicates new five-acre park," 3.

341 *Settlement Agreement,* SVO Pacific Inc. and West Maui Preservation Association, October 24, 2007.

342 *Settlement Agreement,* October 24, 2007, 1.

343 *Settlement Agreement,* October 24, 2007, 1.

Open Space and 150 foot Shoreline Setback Area.[344] WMPA filed a Petition to Intervene in December 2006 and its concerns were noted in the Settlement Agreement:

> WMPA is concerned about the possible cumulative impact of the Lot 3 Expansion Project on traffic, drainage, density, infrastructure, views, noise, the environment, access to public facilities including parks and recreation areas, and has specifically raised certain concerns, and asserted certain claims and positions previously raised in connection with the Special Management Area Use Permits issued by the Commission for the development of Lot 2 by Developer and Lot 4 by a party unrelated to Developer (both lots are part of the Ka'anapali North Beach Subdivision, are adjacent to Lot 3 and subject to the 1988 SMA/SSV Permits as defined below), including its concern, that the methodology being used to count the number of units allowed under the 1988 SMA/SSV Permits is not correct and that a supplemental environmental impact study is required for the development. WMPA has also raised concerns over management and preservation of the dune system, use of beach chairs and other water amenities on the beach, water quality, traffic impacts, adverse noise impacts, infrastructure deficits, public use and access to the Open Space and Shoreline Setback Area and project design.[345]

To address these concerns, this final Settlement Agreement added some of the concessions made with regard to

344 *Settlement Agreement,* October 24, 2007, 3.

345 *Settlement Agreement,* October 24, 2007, 1.

the other lots. The first was extending the Dune Management Program to cover Lot 2 and Lot 3. This program protects the dunes from erosion, maintains the dunes with specific vegetation compatible with the area, and constructs elevated walkways above the dunes. The shoreline setback area was also to be clearly marked, and the 10-acre open space area became known as the "Keka'a Public Open Space/Recreation Area."[346] Besides beach chair and ocean recreation controls, the agreement also mandated that no ocean activities fronting Lot 3 would interfere with canoe practice or canoe regattas. Also, a monk seal and green sea turtle awareness program was instituted—meaning that the developer must be aware of endangered species and not act to impede their space.

As for the ever-present traffic issues, the developer agreed to contribute "$1,680,170.00 toward traffic mitigation on West Maui in satisfaction of Condition 7 of the 1988 SMA/SSV Permits, and Condition cc of the Lot 1 SMA Permit and extension thereof requiring 'other mitigative measures.'"[347] This money was to go towards traffic light synchronization and roadway improvements of Keawe Street. Drainage and water quality monitoring restrictions were also further clarified and restated, and the height of the buildings and specified manner of construction were spelled out. WMPA's website quoted *The Maui News* and Matin as saying that she

---

346 *Settlement Agreement,* October 24, 2007, 8.

347 *Settlement Agreement,* October 24, 2007, 11.

> Was particularly pleased that Intrawest agreed to establish a management plan for the intact sand dune that runs along the shoreline fronting the property and refrain from using pile driving during construction, which can drive neighbors crazy.[348]

Also quoted in this article is Steve Sewall, director of development for Intrawest. He said the "company wanted to work with the public. 'We are a member of the community wherever we go and West Maui is no different.'"[349]

Finally, as with the Benefit Fund established in the Lot 2 Settlement, the Lot 3 Settlement Agreement further clarified the use/function of this Benefit Fund and the method of monetary dispersal to it. WMPA established the community Benefit Fund on September 20, 2007. The developer's obligations were listed as:

> (i) Within thirty (30) days after Developer shall have obtained both (a) final written approval by the Commission of the Special Management Area Use Permit which is the subject of the Lot 3 SMA Permit Application and the applicable appeal period shall have expired without the filing of any appeal or other law suit challenging the terms conditions or issuance of the permit to Developer and (b) the Lot 3 Building Permits, then in such event Developer shall pay to the Benefit Fund the sum of $425,000,

---

348 Valerie Monson, "Condo Project Ok'd: Intervention Assures Kaanapali Plans won't hurt North Beach Dunes," *The Maui News*, February 25, 2005, 1. (http://www.savewestmaui.com/news_mauinews_050225.htm)

349 Valerie Monson, "Condo Project Ok'd: Intervention Assures Kaanapali Plans won't hurt North Beach Dunes," 1.

(ii) Within thirty (30) days after the date of issuance of the first temporary certificate of occupancy for units completed on the Lot 3 Expansion Project, Developer shall pay to the Benefit Fund the sum of $750,000.00;

(iii) Developer shall make the appropriate arrangements for the timeshare owners' association for the Lot 3 Expansion Project to make an annual contribution to the Benefit Fund commencing as of December 31 of the first full calendar year following the year in which the Lot 3 C/O is issued, in an amount equal to $10.00 for each timeshare interval in the Lot 3 Expansion Project sold and closed by Developer as of January 1 of each such year.

(iv) The Benefit Fund shall account for Lot 2 contributions in such a way to ensure compliance with the Lot 2 Settlement Agreement limit.

(v) This continuing contribution shall be stated in the recorded Memorandum of Agreement.[350]

The concessions received by the first intervenors and by WMPA are substantial and many in the community are happy with the results. But, there are still many who are not overjoyed with the (over)development of West Maui, period—development that includes but is not limited to the construction of North Beach. Anthony Pignataro, in an article entitled "Moratorium Time?" noted these agreements as simply "stopgap measures" and pushes the idea that fits his title—that it may be time to put a stop to overall development on West Maui until

350 *Settlement Agreement,* October 24, 2007, 13.

the infrastructure actually has some time to catch up. The article begins:

> Right now the County of Maui is allowing massive commercial and residential construction in West Maui, while new roads to handle their traffic remain at least a decade away. Unless this changes soon, things will get dicey for everyone on the island.[351]

Pignataro quotes a friend as saying that the "'giant yellow birds, the developers' cranes' are 'the official birds of West Maui.' There's at least one in Ka'anapali, but you can find a whole nest of them on North Beach."[352] Former Maui Planning Commissioner Louise Ross wrote in her June 1, 2006 letter to commissioners:

> It is unfortunate that the two massive projects presently underway on North Beach, were allowed to proceed without requiring the developers to participate in sewage treatment plant improvements and traffic abatement measures. Please do not allow these problems to compound by allowing this new project to be built without imposing the above conditions.[353]

Ross is referring to the building of Pulelehua, Maui Land and Pineapple's forthcoming affordable housing project further north in West Maui. The conditions arose from the realization by

---

351 Anthony Pignataro, "Moratorium Time?" *Maui Time Weekly,* Issue 9.52, June 22, 2006. http://savewestmaui.com/news_mauitime_0606.htm.

352 Pignataro, "Moratorium Time?," 2.

353 Pignataro, "Moratorium Time?," 3.

the Maui Planning Commission in 2006 that more infrastructure was indeed needed in West Maui. Pulelehua sidestepped these conditions. This awareness included a push for additional schools and roads. Other roads should also be developed in addition to relying on the construction of the mythical Lahaina Bypass Highway—still many years away from completion. Maui Land and Pineapple started a group called "Bypass Now." This group is looking to another "road in and out of Lahaina."[354] When Maui Land and Pineapple's fortunes failed, Bypass Now closed shop.

This article makes note of something known for years on Maui: very few restrictions and conditions are placed on the developers by the local government. Dick Mayer, retired Maui Community College professor and a member of the Maui General Plan Advisory Committee (GPAC), calls the fees land developers are asked to pay "a joke."[355] Since the article focuses on Pulelehua, and calls for a moratorium on the proposed 882 new affordable housing units for West Maui, it seems odd to call for a halt on building affordable housing because the infrastructure will not allow another development. Why didn't the call for a moratorium come in response to the tourism developments that have always been approved?

Besides the socio-economic and political issues that massive development produces, the fragile environmental balance is

---

354 Pignataro, "Moratorium Time?," 4.

355 Pignataro, "Moratorium Time?," 5.

threatened. And West Maui is no different in this respect to other places marred by seemingly unplanned development. In 2012, Earth Justice representing four community groups Hawai'i Wildlife Fund, Surfrider Foundation, West Maui Preservation Association and Sierra Club-Maui Group, filed a suit under the Clean Water Act against Maui County to limit sewage discharges from injection wells at the Lahaina Wastewater Reclamation Facility.[356]

The groups contend that Maui County should apply for a National Pollutant Discharge Elimination System that would set limits on the amount of pollutants the injection wells are allowed to discharge. "The lawsuit claims that the county knowingly discharges partially treated wastewater into the ocean, and has deliberately chosen not to apply for a federal wastewater discharge permit."[357] Maui County argues that the plant does not require such a permit. But according to these groups, 3 to 5 million gallons of partially treated sewage have been discharged by the injection wells in West Maui near Kahekili Beach Park since at least 2006, causing untold harm to the water supply system, the near shore reefs, and the overall ecosystem.[358]

The groups state that the "freshwater seeps" cause algae blooms to suffocate the coral, and that the treatment facility

356 Mark Veith, "Community groups sue county over sewage discharges," *Lahaina News*, May 3, 2012, 1.

357 "Four community groups sue Maui County over sewage discharge, *The Maui Weekly,* May 3, 2012, 1.

358 Mark Veith, "Community groups sue county over sewage discharges," 1-2.

actually began seeping sewage in 1982 because the subsurface pipe allows the flow to mix with groundwater.[359] Apparently, the "wastewater-derived nitrogen in the algae samples taken over freshwater seeps near Kahekili Beach 'are the highest ever reported in the world.'"[360] The Environmental Protection Agency is beginning to require Maui County to take steps to measure the pollutants. The EPA required the county to disinfect wastewater it discharges, and to "install a nonchlorine disinfection system by 2013."[361]

This is the latest fight to monitor development in this area. And through all the monitoring and negotiations, Keka'a, briefly the capital of the Islands and historically recognized as a wahi pana, a sacred site, has become a modern day example of economic, social and political contestation. More recently, it is the space of massive economic profit for the leaders of industry (sugar, tourism). But, it is the core of the place itself, described and recorded through the generations, that still resonates with those willing and able to sense its magnitude.

---

359 Purna Nemani, "Sewage Plant Accused of Seeping Near Maui Beach," *Courthouse News Service Environmental Law,* April 20, 2012, 1.

360 Purna Nemani, 1.

361 Jennifer Sinco Kelleher, "Groups suing county, allege Lahaina plant damaging reef," *The Associated Press,* April 17, 2012, 1.

Epilogue

At one dollar a page to photocopy documents maintained in the Land Court's public records archive, public assess is compromised. The Land Court file for North Beach consists of thousands of pages of information that pertain to the land titles for Keka'a and for the larger Lahaina District. Lance Collins, on behalf of the Benefit Fund, sought permission from the Land Court to scan and digitize the Land Court file (called an application) for North Beach and all other Land Court applications relating to West Maui land. Because the Land Court is located in Honolulu, the stated intent was to make these documents available for free to the public (and the West Maui community specifically) without having to pay the exorbitant copy charges or the costs of travel to O'ahu.

The initial request to the Registrar of the Land Court was denied and Collins was told to make the request to the Judge of the Land Court. Collins filed such a request: The microfilm reels would be taken from the archive to the court's scanning/ digitizing vendor, scanned, digitized and returned to the archive. The files would then be posted on a public website available for free. This seemed like a logical and easy method to facilitate public access and aid in the research of this entire area. This was not to be. After two court hearings, the Land Court applications have gone nowhere. After making a lengthy list of conditions which the Benefit Fund agreed to, the Judiciary then stated, in a letter, that it was "not able to accommodate [the] request at the present time." The case has languished without a decision by the Court on the request since then.

Who owns the rights to our history? Research is typically challenging in and of itself, and getting to the narratives today is done while navigating through the bureaucratic maze. The information is important because we know who we are by recognizing who we were, and so access to that knowledge is vital for understanding to occur. Historical information offers a view of the self, via the resurrected information obtained from collective and personal pasts. Yi-Fu Tuan says that past reenactment is ended when it lives in the present, and historians reconstruct culture once thought lost, so that we are able to recall and learn from our own yesterdays. Research is the tool to uncovering these narratives that affects us in various ways, as the personal and political intertwine.

Researching land documents is especially important for Hawaiians because what happened to the land is representative of what happened to us—incorporated in power discourses that view ʻāina as capital and kānaka maoli as separated from this source. Reviewing land documents is much more than tracing land title, the information often fills in the larger narratives and aids in an overall understanding of self and other. The unimpeded access to this material is vital and should be encouraged by the court system and the individuals working in this system—those that hold only an artificial claim over the information. This information is public and communal, and should therefore be accessible and affordable to all those willing and wanting to bring forth moʻolelo.

Bibliography

"430 Filipinos Strike on Maui." *Honolulu Star-Bulletin*, June 3, 1937, p. 21, c. 6.

Abercrombie, Neil. Re: *Acceptance of the Final Environmental Impact Statement for the Villages of Leiali'i Affordable Housing Project.* December 7, 2012.

Agreement, H. Hackfield & Co. And H. Turton with James Campbell, July 19, 1880, Book 66, Page 151, Abstract of Title of Pioneer Mill Co. Ltd., In and To Lands of Puou, Euholilea, Kuhua, and Others, Lahiana, Maui, Land Court, Honolulu, Hawai'i.

Agreement, H. Turton to H. Hackfield & Co., August 6, 1884, Book 89, Page 269, Bureau of Conveyances, Honolulu, Hawai'i.

Agreement, Paul Isenberg & H. Hackfield & Co., to James Campbell, July 23, 1884, Book 90, Page, 332. Abstract of Title of Pioneer Mill Co. Ltd., In and To Lands of Puou, Euholilea, Kuhua, and Others, Lahiana, Maui, Land Court, Honolulu, Hawai'i.

"Agreement reached on North Beach time-share project." *The Maui News*, October 6, 1998.

"Amfac/JMB Hawaii L.L.C. History." http://www.fundinguniverse.com/company- histories/amfac-jmb-hawaii-l-l-c-history/.

"An Ode to the Soul." *The Polynesian*, July 11, 1840.

"Attack on 2 Vets, Mate Black Chapter on Maui." *The Honolulu Advertiser*, December 14, 1946, p.1, c.2.

August, Joel E. *Contested Case Hearing: September 22, 1997-October 3, 1997*, Nos. 88/SM1-0123, 88/SSV-002 and SM 970006., Hearing Officer's Report with Proposed Findings of Fact and Conclusions of Law, Decision and Order.

Austin, Tsutumi & Associates, Inc. *Drainage Report for the Honoapiilani Highway Widening Project*, Department of Transportation, Highways Division, State of Hawai'i, January, 1997.

Belt Collins Hawaii Ltd. *Environmental Impact Statement, The Villages of Leiali'i Affordable Housing Project, Lahaina, Maui, Hawai'i*, March 2010.

Carden, Sherri. "Commentary of North Beach." *Haleakalā Times*, July 16-August 5, 1997.

"Case Study No. 5, Industrial Relations Programming, Pioneer Mill Company, Ltd." *Case Study of Effective Industrial Relations Case Study No. 1, Employee Information Program Hawaiian Pineapple Co., Ltd.* Honolulu, 1951.

Chenoweth, David. *Testimony before the Maui County Council Regarding the West Maui Community Plan Update*, September 26, 1995.

Collins, Lance. email correspondense, September 15, 2013.

Collins to Hedani. *Maui Planning Commission Requesting an Account of the Disbursement of Funds to West Maui Preservation Association from Maui Beach LP*, April 17, 2007.

Cooper, George & Daws, Gavan. *Land and Power in Hawai'i: The Democratic Years*. Honolulu: University of Hawai'i Press, 1990.

Community Plan Update, Proposed West Maui Community Plan. Maui Planning Department, September, 1993.

Contested Case Hearing: September 22, 1997-October 3, 1997. Findings of Fact, Conclusions of Law, Decision and Order, Nos. 88/SM1-023, 88/SSV-002, and SM1 970006. County of Maui, State of Hawai'i, October 28, 1988.

Dames & Moore, *Environmental Assessment for Department of the Army Permit Application, North Beach, Ka'anapali.* Kaanapali North Beach Joint Venture, June 10, 1987.

Dawson, Donnie. "Amfac: New and Improved? The former Big Five company goes Entrepreneurial." *Island Business,* August 1997, 17-22.

Deed, James Campbell to Henry Turton, June 16, 1877. Abstract of Title of Pioneer Mill Co. Ltd., In and To Lands of Puou, Euholilea, Kuhua, and Others, Lahiana, Maui, Land Court, Honolulu, Hawai'i.

DeNaie, Lucienne. "The proposed new development at North Beach-Part 2: Environmental impacts and 'mitigation.'" *Haleakalā Times,* March 5-18, 1997.

Donham, Theresa K. & Rosenthal, Paul H., Ph.D., "Data Recovery Excavations at the Honokahua Burial Site, Land of Honokahua, Lahaina District, Island of Maui." Prepared for Kapalua Land Company, Ltd., Hilo, Hawai'i, 2000.

Dorrance, William H. *Sugar Islands: The 165-year Story of Sugar in Hawai'i.* Honolulu: Mutual Publishing, 2000.

Eager, Harry. "Agreement reached on N. Beach: Faction opposing time-share project 'happy' with terms." *The Maui News,* October 6, 1998.

Eager, Harry. "Intrawest's second tower of new Honua Kai slated for 2010." *The Maui News,* February 6, 2009.

Eager, Harry. "Kaanapali Ocean Villas time share deferred for more talks." *The Maui News,* August 25, 2004.

Eager, Harry. "North Beach deal could be in the making: Council hears from mayor on idea to buy one-third of property." *The Maui News*, July 8, 1997.

Eager, Harry. "N. Beach settlement called 'wonderful.'" *The Maui News*, October 14, 1998.

Eager, Harry. "North Beach SMA rejected—but not quite finally." *The Maui News*, October 20, 1998.

Eager, Harry. "Planning Commission hears terms and reasons for pact." *The Maui News*, October 14, 1998.

Environmental Impact Statement, The Villages of Leiali'i Affordable Housing Project. Lahaina, Maui, Hawai'i, March 2010.

Findings and Order Denying Petition for Writ of Quo Warranto. Second Circuit Court, Sate of Hawaii, January 10, 2008.

Findings of Fact, Conclusions of Law, Decision and Order. Contested Case Hearing: September 22, 1997-October 3, 1997. Nos. 88/SM1-023, 88/SSV-002 and SM1 970006. Maui Planning Commission, Hawai'i,

Fitzpatrick, Gary L. "Mapmaking at Lahainaluna." In *He Mau Palapala Aina, A Me Na Niele e Pili Ana: Maps and Questions Regarding Them*. Honolulu: Hawaiian Historical Society, 2011.

Fornander, Abraham. *Fornander Collection of Hawaiian Antiquities and Folk-Lore*. Memoirs of the Bernice Pauahi Bishop Museum, Vols. 4, 5, 6. Honolulu:Bishop Museum Press, 1916-1917.

"Four community groups sue Maui County over sewage discharge. *The Maui Weekly*, May 3, 2012.

Freeman, Paul. "Abandoned and little known airfields: Hawaii, Maui Island." http://airfileds-freeman.com/HI/Airfields_HI_Maui.htm, 2001.

Fujii, Jocelyn. *Kapalua Nui: Place of Life*. Honolulu: Hula Moon Press, 2008.

"General Correspondence, Incoming Letters of the Board of Education 1896, Maui, June-August." 261-33-2. Hawai'i State Archives, Honolulu, Hawai'i.

Goldman, Rita. "Embracing the Past." *Embrace*. Kapalua, 2005.

Grant of Easement and Agreement Regarding Allocation of Retention Capacity, North Beach—Mauka Retention Basins. Land Court TMK No. (2)4-4-2:039 (POR), October 20, 2004.

Handy, E. S. Craighill. *The Hawaiian Planter: His Plants, Methods and Areas of Cultivation, Vol 1*. Bernice P. Bishop Museum Bulletin 161. Honolulu: The Bishop Museum, 1940.

Hawaii Sugar Planters Association Archives (HSPA), Hamilton Library, University of Hawai'i, Mānoa.

Register of the Pioneer Mill Company Lahaina, Maui, 1873-1960. "Pioneer
Company History."

1-2 PMC "Agreements, Miscellaneous."

0-1-3 PMC "Personnel & Payroll: Sept.-Dec. 1937 & 1938."

0-1-4 PMC "Balance Sheets, Annual 1916-1935."

PMC 0-1-6 "Honokohau Water Costs August 30, 1919-Sept. 30, 1928."

1-14 PMC "Census of Sugar Workers, HSPA 1927-1029, 1935-1941."

1-16 PMC "Comparative Costs: Labor, 1930-1933."

PMC "Maui Summary HSPA Census June 30, 1939."

Hawn Hd 9109.P56A37, HSPA Archives, Hamilton Library, University of Hawai'i, Mānoa.

"Report of the Pioneer Mill Co. Ltd. for Fifteen Months Ending December 31,
1901."

"Report of the Pioneer Mill Co. Ltd. for Fifteen Months Ending December 31, 1903."
"Report of the Pioneer Mill Co. Ltd. for Fifteen Months Ending December 31, 1904."
"Report of the Pioneer Mill Co. Ltd. for Fifteen Months Ending December 31, 1909."
"Report of the Pioneer Mill Co. Ltd. for Fifteen Months Ending December 31, 1910."
"Report of the Pioneer Mill Co. Ltd. for Fifteen Months Ending December 31, 1911."
"Report of the Pioneer Mill Co. Ltd. for Fifteen Months Ending December 31, 1912."
"Report of the Pioneer Mill Co. Ltd. for Fifteen Months Ending December 31, 1913."
"Report of the Pioneer Mill Co. Ltd. for Fifteen Months Ending December 31, 1917."
"Report of the Pioneer Mill Co. Ltd. for Fifteen Months Ending December 31, 1919."

Helber, Hastert, and Kimura, Planners. *North Beach Kaanapali Draft Environmental Impact Statement.* Planning Department, County of Maui, Hawai'i, August 1987.

Hawaiian Annual for 1908.

Helber, Hastert, and Kimura, Planners. *North Beach Kaanapali Final Environmental Impact Statement*, Planning Department, County of Maui, Hawai'i, October 1987.

"HFDC Must Pay Amfac $750,000 to Leave Unencumbered State Land, Bond Says." *Environment Hawai'i*, Aug. 1, 1994 v. 5 n. 2.

Hiraga, Gwen Ohashi. Project Manager, *Re: Special Management Area Use Permit and Step 2 Planned Development Applications for the Proposed Honua Kai Resort, North Beach and Related Improvements*, Report to Maui Planning Commission, March 1, 2007.

"Home Ownership Being Pushed by Pioneer Mill Co." *Honolulu Star-Bulletin*, May 2, 1950, p. 20, c. 4.

Howland, Mark A. Chief Biologist, Environmental Research Corps. "Can North Beach Be Saved?" 1997.

Howland, Mark A. Chief Biologist, Environmental Research Corps, *Commentary to the Maui Planning Commission in response to the proposed Ka'anapali Ocean Resorts by AMFAC Maui*, August 25, 1997.

Interview with Jo Anne Johnson, Director of Transportation, Maui County, January 18, 2013.

Interview with Joel E. August, September 2013.

Interview with Randy Draper, Napili, Hawai'i, April 10, 2013.

Jacoby, Andrew. "North Beach Venture hotel plans could be bogged down in wetlands." *Maui Tribune*, Vol. 1, Issue 18, April 12, 1995.

James, Van. *Ancient Sites of Maui, Moloka'i, and Lāna'i: Archaeological Places of Interest in the Hawaiian Islands*. Honolulu: Mutual Publishing, 2001.

Jensen, Peter M. *Archaeological Inventory Survey Lahaina Master Planned Project Site, Land of Wahikuli, Lahaina District, Island of Maui*, October 1989.

Johnson, Jo Anne. Director of Transportation, Maui County. Interview, January 18, 2013.

Johnson, Jeanne Booth. "Ancient Land." *Honolulu Advertiser*, Hawaiian Holiday, Aug. 30, 1959.

Johnson, Jeanne Booth. "Maui's Past Shown in Stone." *Honolulu Advertiser*, Hawaiian Holiday, Dec. 7, 1958.

Kamakau, Samuel Manaiakalani. "Ka Moolelo o Hawaii." Translated by E.P. Sterling. *Ke Au Okoa*, March 10, 1870.

Kanepuu, J.J. He Moolelo no Pakaa, *Ke Au Okoa*, Oct. 17, 1867.

Ke Au Hou. September 21, 1910. MS SC Sterling 3.12.3.

"Kekaa Open Space Recreational Area dedicated." *The Maui News*, January 16, 2002,

Kelleher, Jennifer Sinco. "Groups suing county, allege Lahaina plant damaging reef." *The Associated Press*, April 17, 2012.

Kent, Noel. *Hawai'i: Islands Under the Influence*. Honolulu: University of Hawai'i Press, (1983) 1993.

King, R.D. "Districts in the Hawaiian Islands in J. W. Coulter." *A Gazetteer of the Territory of Hawaii*. Honolulu: University of Hawai'i Press, 1935.

Kyselka, Will & Lanterman, Ray. *Maui: How It Came to Be*. Honolulu: University of Hawai'i Press, 1980.

Land Commission Award 76, Volume 1, page 225-230, Bureau of Conveyances, Honolulu, Hawai'i.

Land Court Applications, Applicant Pioneer Mill Company, Ltd., Original Certificate of Title No. 80,096, Application No. 1744, Bureau of Conveyances, Honolulu, Hawai'i.

Land Deed, P. Shaw & wife To H. Turton, Book 62, Page 46-47, Bureau of Conveyances, Honolulu, Hawai'i.

Lecker, George Theodore. "Lahainaluna, 1831-1877: A Study of the History of Hawaii's Pioneer Educational Institution and Its Socio-economic Influence at Home and Abroad." Thesis, Master of Arts, University of Hawaii, 1938.

Legal Description of Lots 1-4 of Ka'anapali North Beach, Exhibit D.

Letter from David W. Blane to John Akana, Chair and Members Maui Planning Commission. Re: Kaanapali North Beach Joint Venture, December 6, 1996.

Letter from George C. Montgomery to Mr. Blanco Re: Puukolii Village AMFAC.

Letter from Jo Anne Johnson and Randy Draper to Teney K. Takahashi, June 4, 1997.

Letter from Jo Anne Johnson to Wayne Nishiki, Maui County Council, October 2, 1996.

Letter from Linda Crockett Lingle to Jo Anne Johnson Subject: Proposed Puukoliii Village Development, September 16, 1996.

Letter from Patsy T. Mink to The Honorable James V. Hansen, Chair House Resources Subcommittee on National Parks and Public Lands, June 5, 1997.

Letter from Teney K. Takahashi, Senior Vice President Amfac, to Randy Draper, June 27, 1997.

Letter from Teney K. Takahashi, Senior Vice President Amfac, to Jo Anne Johnson and Randy Draper, May 30, 1997.

Martin, W.F. & Pierce, C.H. "Water Resources of Hawaii 1909-1911." Department of the Interior, United States Geological Survey. Washington: Washington Printing Office, 1913.

Maui Land & Pineapple Company records.

Maui Planning Commission, Minutes—February 28, 2006, p. 33-63.

Maui Planning Commission Minutes—March 13, 2007, p. 92-118.

Maui Planning Commision Minutes—May 28, 2013, p. 38-48.

McConkey, J.F. *The Maui News*, Oct. 18, 1969.

Mink, Patsy. H.R. 576, 105th Congress, 1st Session, "To direct the Secretary of the Interior to undertake the necessary feasibility studies regarding the establishment of certain new units of the National Park System in the State of Hawaii."

Moffat, Riley M. & Fitzpatrick, Gary L. *Mapping the Lands and Waters of Hawai'i: The Hawaiian Government Survey, Palapala'aina, Vol. 3*. Honolulu: Editions Limited, 2004.

Monson, Valerie. "Condo Project Ok'd: Intervention Assures Kaanapali Plans won't hurt North Beach Dunes." *The Maui News*, February 25, 2005. (http://www.savewestmaui.com/news_mauinews_050225.htm)

Monson, Valerie. "North Beach struggle put on shelf for a month: Parties to SMA permit case look for agreement." *The Maui News*, May 13, 1998, A3.

Mortgage, Henry Turton to James Campbell, June 16, 1877, Vol. 51, Page 24. Abstract of Title of PioneerMill Co. Ltd., In and To Lands of Puou, Euholilea, Kuhua, and Others, Lahiana, Maui, Land Court, Honolulu, Hawai'i.

Mortgage, Henry Turton to H. Hackfield & Co., Abstract of Title of Pioneer Mill Co. Ltd., In and To Lands of Puou, Euholilea, Kuhua, and Others, Lahiana, Maui, Land Court, Honolulu, Hawai'i.

Mortgage Deed, H. Turton to H. Hackfield, Bureau of Conveyances, Honolulu, Hawai'i.Book 86, Page 244-258, 245.

Munekiyo & Arakawa, Inc. *Application for Special Management Area Use Permit,Ka'anapali Ocean Resort*, March 1997.

Munekiyo & Arakawa, Inc. *Final Environmental Assessment (EISPN), Kaanapali Vacation Club*, August 1996.

Munekiyo & Hiraga, Inc. *Kaanapali 2020 Plan, Environmental Impact Statement Preparation Notice*, February 2005.

Munekiyo & Hiraga, Inc. *Special Management Area Use Permit and Step 2 Planned Development Applications for the Proposed Honua Kai Resort, North Beach Park and Related Improvements*. March 7, 2007.

Munekiyo & Suyama to Deputy Director Colleen Suyama, *Honua Kai Resort—Proposed Restaurant Revisions*, November 21, 2007.

Nellist, George F., edited by. "The Story of Hawaii and Its Builders." *Honolulu Star-*

Bulletin, Hawaii, 1925.

Nemani, Purna. "Sewage Plant Accused of Seeping Near Maui Beach." *Courthouse News Service Environmental Law*, April 20, 2012.

"New Names for 4 Isle Waterfalls." *Honolulu Advertiser*, Oct. 1, 1969, D4.

"Nine Pioneer Mill Employes Let Out (sic)." *Honolulu Star-Bulletin*, November 21, 1946, p.1, C. 4.

Nogelmeier, Puakea M. "Hawaiian Geography, Old and New" In *He Mau Palapala Aina, A Me Na Niele e Pili Ana: Maps and Questions Regarding Them*. Honolulu: Hawaiian Historical Society, 2011.

"Obituary, Death of Henry Turton, Sr.," *The Daily Herald*, Honolulu, Hawaiian Islands, July 11, 1887.

Office of Hawaiian Affairs v. Housing and Community Development Corporation of Hawai'i (HCDCH), In the Supreme Court of the State of Hawai'i, No. 25570, Appeal From the First Circuit Court, October 27, 2009.

Option to Purchase, Amfac Property Investment Corp. to County of Maui, September 19, 1997.

PBR Hawaii, *Final Environmental Impact Report, Puukolii Village, Volume II*, January 1993.

Perry, Brian. "Panel balks at action on North Beach, Question raised on objectivity of county lawyers." *The Maui News*, October 29, 1997.

Petition for Writ of Quo Warranto, Second Circuit Court, State of Hawaii, January 10, 2008.

Anthony Pignataro, *Maui Time Weekly*, July 5, 2007.

Pignataro, Anthony. "Moratorium Time?" *Maui Time Weekly*, Issue 9.52, June 22, 2006. http://savewestmaui.com/news_mauitime_0606.htm.

Pioneer Mill Company: A Maui Sugar Plantation Legacy. Center for Oral History, Social Science Research Institute. Honolulu: University of Hawai'i, Mānoa, December 2003.

James Higuchi Oral Interview.
Fred Higuchi, Oral History Interview.
Edward Hussey: Biographical Summary.
Kazukiyo "Jiggs" Kuboyama, Biographical Summary.

"Pioneer Mill Co. Workers' Attack Cases Continued." *The Honolulu Advertiser*, December 21, 1946, p. 4., c. 5.

"Pioneer Mill Estimates Loss at $700,000." *Honolulu Star-Bulletin*, January 1, 1947, p. 5, c. 8.

"Pioneer Mill in Stalemate Over Firings." *The Honolulu Advertiser*, p. 3, c. 6.

Pioneer Mill News Bulletin, April 1976-October 1982. (inc.). April 4, 1979. Hamilton Library, University of Hawai'i, Mānoa.

Pioneer Mill News Bulletin, April 1976-October 1982. (inc.). July 9, 1979. Hamilton Library, University of Hawai'i, Mānoa.

Pioneer Mill News Bulletin, April 1976-October 1982. (inc.). July 16, 1979. Hamilton Library, University of Hawai'i, Mānoa.

Pioneer Mill News Bulletin, April 1976-October 1982. (inc.). February 14, 1980. Hamilton Library, University of Hawai'i, Mānoa.

Pioneer Mill News Bulletin, April 1976-October 1982. (inc.). October 7, 1980 Hamilton Library, University of Hawai'i, Mānoa.

Pioneer Mill News Bulletin, April 1976-October 1982. (inc.). February 6, 1981. Hamilton Library, University of Hawai'i, Mānoa.

Pioneer Mill News Bulletin, April 1976-October 1982. (inc.). September 19, 1981. Hamilton Library, University of Hawai'i, Mānoa.

"Pioneer Mill Workers In Virtual CIO Slavery." *The Honolulu Advertiser*, December 16, 1946, p. 1, c. 3.

"Pioneer to Sell House Lots." *The Honolulu Advertiser*, April 5, 1950, p. 19, c. 2.

Pukui, Mary Kawena & Elbert, Samuel H. *Hawaiian Dictionary*. Honolulu: University of Hawai'i Press, (1957) 1986.

Randy Draper interview, Napili, Hawaii, April 10, 2013.

Rockett, Louise. "Honua Kai dedicates new five-acre park." *Lahaina News*, February 11, 2010.

Ruel, Tim. "Dynsasty in decline: Amfac, the first Hawaii company to earn $1 billion in revenue, is a shadow of its former self." *Honolulu Star-Bulletin*, September 2, 2001.

Settlement Agreement, relating to Kaanapali North Beach, Docket Nos. SM 970006, 88/SM1-023 and 88/SSV-002, Maui Planning Commission, State of Hawaii, September 24, 1998.

Settlement Agreement, SVO Pacific, Inc., and the West Maui Preservation Association, September 2004.

Settlement Agreement, Maui Beach Resort Limited Partnership and The West Maui Preservation Association, Inc. February 2, 2005.

Sterling, Elspeth P. *Sites of Maui, A. Fornander Collection*. Honolulu: Bishop Museum Press, 1998.

Stevens, Tom. "West Maui—AMFAC's North Beach; condos a-comin, Lingle calls Patsy Mink's North Beach park proposal 'hollow.'" *Haleakalā Times*, July 16-August 5, 1997.

Stipulation to Proposed Findings of Fact, Conclusions of Law, Decision and Order, Contested Case Hearings, September 22, 1997-October 3, 1997. Maui Planning Commission, State of Hawaii, September 29, 1998.

"Strike Strategy of ILWU Planned In Detail On Maui." *The Honolulu Advertiser*, December 15, 1946, p. 1, c. 7.

Takahashi, Teney K. Amfac Senior Vice President, Amfac Letter, December 26, 1996.

Takaki, Ronald. *Pau Hana: Plantation Life and Labor in Hawaii*. Honolulu: University of Hawai'i Press, 1983.

Thrum, Thomas G. *Hawaiian Annual for 1908*. Honolulu: Black & Auld, Printers, 1923.

Unilateral Declaration of Restrictions, North Beach Unit Count and Drainage. Amfac Property Investment Corp. (APIC), October 7, 1998.

Urry, John. *The Tourist Gaze*. Thousand Oaks, California: Sage Publications, 1990.

Veith, Mark. "Beach access, cap on units part of pact on North Beach resort." *Lahaina News*. Vol. 19, No. 41.

Veith, Mark. "Community groups sue county over sewage discharges." *Lahaina News*, May 3, 2012.

Veith, Mark. "Hearing officer recommends approval for new time share at North Beach." *Lahaina News*, Vol. 19, No. 2, January 8-January 14, 1998.

Veith, Mark. "Mayor and Council Discuss Stances on North Beach." *Lahaina News*, Vol. 18, No. 28, July 10-July 16, 1997.

Veith, Mark. "North Beach Issues to be Dissected in Lengthy

Hearings." *Lahaina News*, Vol. 18, No. 29, July 17-July 23, 1997.

"Voting Today, Work Return Set Thursday." *The Honolulu Advertiser*, December 30, 1946, p. 1, c. 6.

Walker, William Metcalf. *Archaeology of Maui: draft report, sketches, and plates*. MS SC Walker Box 1: ff MS SC Box 2.

Whitney, Henry M. "Rural Sketches of the Hawaiian Islands, Lahaina Revisited." *The Pacific Commercial Advertiser*, March 26, 1864.

Withdrawal of Intervenors JoAnne Johnson and James Johnson; Certificate of Service, Contested Case Hearings September 22, 1997-October 3, 1997, Maui Planning Commission, September 29, 1998.

Youn, Jacy L. "Cropped Down." *hawaiibusiness.com*.

Appendix A

LINDA LINGLE
GOVERNOR

JAMES R. AIONA, JR.
LIEUTENANT GOVERNOR

STATE OF HAWAII
OFFICE OF THE LIEUTENANT GOVERNOR
OFFICE OF INFORMATION PRACTICES
NO. 1 CAPITOL DISTRICT BUILDING
250 SOUTH HOTEL STREET, SUITE 107
HONOLULU, HAWAI'I 96813
Telephone: (808) 586-1400 FAX: (808) 586-1412
E-MAIL: oip@hawaii.gov
www.hawaii.gov/oip

LESLIE H. KONDO
DIRECTOR

OPINION

Requester: West Maui Preservation Association, Inc.
Board: Maui Planning Commission
Date: June 27, 2007
Subject: Right to Present Testimony (S RFO-P 07-23)

REQUEST FOR OPINION

Requester, through its attorney, seeks a determination as to whether the Maui Planning Commission (the "Commission") violated the Sunshine Law, part I of chapter 92, Hawaii Revised Statutes ("HRS"), during its meeting held on March 13, 2007. Although Requester asks that OIP opine on four specific questions, based upon the information provided by Requester and the Commission, OIP does not believe that the issues as framed by Requester need be addressed.[1] Rather, after reviewing the submissions, the question for OIP's consideration is simply whether the Commission denied a member of the public the right to testify during the meeting.

Unless otherwise indicated, this opinion is based solely upon the facts presented in Requester's letters to OIP dated March 15, April 11, and May 3, 2007, the letter from Ms. Colleen M. Suyama, Deputy Director of the Department of Planning,[2] to OIP dated March 22, 2007, and documents that were provided to OIP under cover of those letters. Those documents include the agenda for the

---

[1] Requester's allegations about the actions of the Commission's staff are outside of OIP's jurisdiction. Likewise, Requester's complaint about the lack of courtesy that the Commission and/or its staff extended to testifiers is not a Sunshine Law issue except insofar as it relates to the question of whether the Commission deprived a member of the public of the right to testify.

[2] OIP understands Ms. Suyama, as the Planning Director's designee, served as Commission staff at the meeting and that her response to OIP is made on behalf of the Commission.

OIP Op. Ltr. No. 07-10

Commission's March 13 meeting, a verbatim transcript relating to the Commission's consideration of the relevant agenda item and Ms. Sharyn Matin's oral testimony relating to that item, and a video recording of the meeting.

QUESTIONS PRESENTED

1. Whether a board may restrict public testimony to the subject matter the board intended an agenda item to cover, when the subject matter listed for the item on the filed agenda can reasonably be read to include proffered testimony.

2. Whether the Commission restricted Ms. Matin from presenting testimony relating to an agenda item, in violation of the Sunshine Law.

BRIEF ANSWERS

1. No. A board may not restrict testifiers from testifying on issues that relate to an agenda item, and it must broadly interpret the agenda item for the purpose of determining whether testimony is related to the agenda item. The scope of an agenda item is determined by the language used on the filed agenda, not the board's intent as to the meaning of the agenda item.

2. Yes. The transcript and video recording of the meeting reflect that Ms. Suyama, acting on behalf of the Commission, asked Ms. Matin to limit her testimony to a narrower range of issues than the agenda item reasonably encompassed. Through its accedence to Ms. Suyama's limitation of Ms. Matin's testimony, the Commission violated the Sunshine Law's public testimony requirement. However, the violation does not appear to have been intentional.

FACTS

The Commission's agenda for its March 13 meeting included under the heading "Communications":[3]

> 1. MAUI BEACH LIMITED PARTNERSHIP submitting their annual report on the disbursement of the funds in the Settlement Agreement between developer and the WEST MAUI PRESERVATION ASSOCIATION, INC. . . . .

The report itself was not a part of the agenda.

---

[3] OIP notes that the agenda's description of the item under the heading "Communications" may be somewhat misleading to the public. OIP strongly recommends that the agenda be written more accurately to convey that the Commission intends to consider the report, instead of the communication transmitting the report, by not placing the item under such a heading.

During the developer's report, the Commission asked Ms. Matin to come up and answer questions about delays in the formation of a nonprofit organization to receive funds from the developer as outlined in the settlement agreement.[4] Ms. Matin's discussion of that matter was in response to the Commission's request, rather than a presentation of her own testimony. Nonetheless, it appears from the transcript that the Commission was ready to move on to other items after extensively questioning Ms. Matin about the formation of the nonprofit, perhaps under the impression that her testimony was complete. However, Ms. Matin reminded the Commission that she had not yet presented her testimony on the noticed subject matter. The Commission then indicated that she could proceed with her testimony.

After Ms. Matin began to testify concerning the developer's disbursements to meet other requirements of the settlement, Ms. Suyama[5] interrupted her several times and asked her to limit her testimony to the disbursement of funds in the settlement agreement, which she defined to be "specific monetary requirements that were identified" and "how those monies were being disbursed finally by the developer to the various organizations." Ms. Suyama argued with Ms. Matin about the scope of the agenda item and Ms. Matin ultimately limited the scope of her testimony to the subject matter Ms. Suyama had identified.

DISCUSSION

The Sunshine Law requires the Commission to allow any member of the public an opportunity to present oral testimony on any item on its agenda. Haw. Rev. Stat. § 92-3 (1993). The Commission can require that the testimony be related to the agenda item, but it cannot otherwise restrict or censor a person's testimony. WMPA asserts that Ms. Matin was not allowed to testify on information that she believed was required to be included in the report that was being presented to the Commission under the agenda item in question. The issue here, thus, is whether Ms. Matin's proffered testimony was, in fact, related to the agenda item listed.

Because the developer's report was not part of the agenda, the public was only notified of the general subject matter expected to be covered by the report but not the specifics of what the report actually included. Given this notice, the Commission could not restrict public testimony to the items actually presented in the developer's report. Rather, it could only properly limit testimony to the report's

---

4 Although the matter was certainly not the central subject listed on the agenda, it was sufficiently related to the subject matter of the report to allow the Commission to ask questions about it under the report.

5 Ms. Suyama is not a member of the Commission, but was acting as Commission staff at the meeting and spoke with the apparent concurrence of the Commission. OIP therefore imputes her actions and intent to the Commission.

announced general subject matter, namely: "the disbursement of the funds in the Settlement Agreement."

From the transcript and the video recording, it appears that the Commission (as represented by Ms. Suyama) interpreted the agenda item to mean only those disbursements by the developer for which a specific sum was required in the settlement agreement. The Commission's restriction of Ms. Matin's testimony was based on an overly narrow reading of the agendized subject matter.

To carry out the Sunshine Law's intent, OIP is statutorily required to liberally construe the law's provisions to favor open meetings and to strictly limit the exceptions to the general rule of open meetings. See Haw. Rev. Stat. § 92-1 (1993).[6] Consistent with these instructions, OIP must construe the public's right to "present oral testimony on any agenda item" liberally to favor public testimony. Haw. Rev. Stat. § 92-3. Thus, where it is at least arguable that an agenda item could be read to cover a particular issue, a board must accept proffered testimony on that issue. Further, a board must determine the relevant subject matter based on the specific wording it used on the agenda and may not add additional limitations or phrases after the fact in exercising its power to require that testimony be limited to the agenda item at hand.

Under that standard, OIP cannot conclude that Ms. Matin's proffered testimony on conditions of the settlement agreement that she believed would require the developer to spend money was unrelated to the subject matter noticed by the agenda item. Clearly, Ms. Matin read "disbursement of the funds in the Settlement Agreement" more broadly than did Ms. Suyama on behalf of the Commission, but Ms. Matin's reading was not an unreasonable one given the agenda item listed.

At the same time, though, a board does not necessarily violate the Sunshine Law by asking questions of a testifier or letting a testifier know what aspect of an

---

[6] The first section of the Sunshine Law states that:

> (1) It is the intent of [the Sunshine Law] to protect the people's right to know;
>
> (2) The provisions requiring open meetings shall be liberally construed; and
>
> (3) The provisions providing for exceptions to the open meeting requirements shall be strictly construed against closed meetings.

Id.

agenda item is of particular interest to the board. Indeed, since those who testify generally seek to persuade the board and have a limited time to do so, it is likely that many testifiers would welcome such guidance. Based on both the transcript and the video recording of the meeting, OIP concludes that Ms. Suyama may have intended to guide Ms. Matin toward the issues of particular interest to the board rather than to prohibit her from testifying on the issues she had first raised.[7] However, Ms. Suyama's instruction regarding the scope of the agenda item did have the effect of restricting Ms. Matin's ability to testify. This restriction violated the Sunshine Law, but it is OIP's opinion that the violation was not intentional.

In summary, the Commission may not restrict testifiers from testifying on issues that fall within the general subject matter of an agenda item. Although the Commission can require that testimony be related to the agenda item, the Commission must interpret the agenda item broadly for the purpose of determining whether testimony is related to the agenda item.

RIGHT TO BRING SUIT

Any person may file a lawsuit to require compliance with or to prevent a violation of the Sunshine Law or to determine the applicability of the Sunshine Law to discussions or decisions of a government board. Haw. Rev. Stat. § 92-12 (1993). The court may order payment of reasonable attorney fees and costs to the prevailing party in such a lawsuit. Id.

OFFICE OF INFORMATION PRACTICES

Jennifer Z. Brooks
Staff Attorney

APPROVED:

Leslie H. Kondo
Director

---

7 WMPA asks OIP to address separately the issue of Ms. Suyama's demeanor toward Ms. Matin during this interchange, which WMPA argues was inappropriately badgering and berating in tone and constituted a tirade. OIP concludes that Ms. Suyama's tone of voice was at most testy, and while that is relevant to the issue of whether Ms. Suyama's statements reasonably had the effect of restricting Ms. Matin's testimony, it does not create a separate issue for OIP's review.

Appendix B

LAW OFFICE OF
LANCE D COLLINS
A LAW CORPORATION

Post Office Box 179336, Honolulu, Hawaii 96817
808.243.9292 • lawyer@maui.net

October 3, 2013

Ivan Lay, Chair
Maui Planning Commission
250 S. High Street
Wailuku, HI 96793

Re: Condition No. 32 of the Special Management Area Use Permit and Step 2 Planned Development approvals for the proposed Honua Kai Resort, North Beach Park, and related improvements at TMK: 4-4-014: 006 and 008, and 4-4-001: 010, Kaanapali, Lahaina, Island of Maui. (SM1 2004/0017) (PD2 2004/0005) (J. Prutch)

Dear Chair Lay and Commissioners,

I represent the West Maui Preservation Association (WMPA). In reviewing the minutes of the May 28, 2013 meeting, WMPA would like to set the record straight regarding a number of factually erroneous statements made regarding the aforementioned SMA permit and the settlement agreement.

The settlement agreement between WMPA and the Developer regarding the Lot 4 SMA permit (hereafter "Settlement Agreement) is a public document that was filed with the Commission in February, 2005.

Condition No. 32 of the SMA permit required the Developer to annually report on disbursements of funds pursuant to the Settlement Agreement. Under the Settlement Agreement, WMPA received two disbursements in 2005 and there are no other disbursements that will be made to WMPA. These disbursements, which occurred in 2005, are reported every year to the Commission as having been disbursed in 2005.

At the May 28, 2013 meeting, Planner Joe Prutch stated:

> Mr. Joe Prutch: Good afternoon everybody. This is the Honua Kai Annual Report, part of the Settlement Agreement. The Planned Development and the SM1 was approved back in 2005. One of the conditions is that an annual report shall be filed with the Maui Planning Commission on the disbursement of the funds in the settlement agreements for your information. There used to be two intervenors. It was Charlie Fox and WMPA. Charlie Fox funds have all been paid in full I think two years ago. We're pau with Charlie Fox, but the WMPA money is still being paid. So far what I have calculated is the amount to be disbursed to WMPA was about 2.1 million. The amount disbursed so far is about 1.2, so there's still about $887,000 remains and from last year's report to this year's report, I saw that it was about $192,000 was paid for the Mill Street Extension Traffic Study. Gwen's not here, but Colleen Suyama is here from Munekiyo, so she's gonna come up and give you a report and

1

she'll be able to answer any questions and she has a representative from Honua Kai here as well. I didn't get his name, but he'll mention his name when he comes up. Thank you. (38)

Mr. Prutch's statement regarding millions of dollars going to WMPA is factually erroneous. Under the Settlement Agreement, the only amounts WMPA was to receive was "up to" $25,000 (and actually $24,513 to Isaac D. Hall, Esq.) for reimbursement of its attorney's fees related to the contested case and mediation process and a $100,000 donation. Both of these disbursements occurred in 2005 and have been reported annually since then to the Commission.

Under Paragraph 8 of the Settlement Agreement, the Developer is obligated to contribute $2,500,000 for traffic impacts including the additional lane along the Lower Honoapiilani Road, improvements to the Honoapiilani Highway between the Lower Honoapiilani Road and Halawai Drive, traffic light sychronization, the Mill Street extension, and design studies for the Lahaina Bypass Highway north of Keawe Street). None of these monies are disbursed to WMPA and WMPA receives no portion of the monies. It is WMPA's understanding that some of these monies have been disbursed at the direction of the State and the County to particular contractors and "study" consultants as more particularly described in previous annual reports and that some monies remain to be disbursed.

Ms. Suyama, who was the planner assigned to this SMA permit during the initial intervention and approval process, and now is a private planner for this project stated at the May 28, 2013 meeting:

> The other money, the sales money that we're talking about goes directly to WMPA. That was part of the settlement agreement that they get these funds from the sales and the resales of the unit and it's basically funding the West Maui Preservation Association which Intrawest has no control over. (41)

Mr. Sewall, the Developer's representative, also stated:

> So but I know those funds are still being distributed to WMPA, but I've got no knowledge of, you know, any use of those funds to date. So I don't know what they've been spending the money on, but it was more than just that 25 percent. We gave them a fairly significant amount of start up cash or whatever you wanna call it at the time that the settlement was done as well. (45-46)

These statements are factually erroneous. Under Paragraph 9 of the Settlement Agreement, the Developer was required to disburse funds to a separate charitable non-profit established, jointly by WMPA and the Developer, for projects benefiting the West Maui community. It is that organization that Mr. Sewall and Ms. Suyama are referred to. That organization includes on its board one seat for a WMPA representative and one seat for a Developer's representative, the remaining seats are for community members (and in the past have included the Commission's own former member Dr. William Iaconetti), as required by the Settlement Agreement. Since it's creation until early last year, the Developer has had a representative serve on that Board: Mr. Eric Gerlach, Mr. Anthony Plitt, then Mr. Mike Walker.

That other entity is funded by a transfer fee imposed on resales as required by the Settlement Agreement and recorded against each unit. None of those monies are disbursed to WMPA and

2

WMPA receives no portion of the transfer fees. It is WMPA's understanding that the Developer controls the owner's association and would therefore be in the best position to know when resales have occurred.

As Mr. Sewall also said, the Developer's interactions with WMPA have been limited and have involved disputes over enforcement of the settlement agreement:

> You know, we still have dealing with them on time to time on issues they don't think that we're actually maybe conforming to specifically the letter of the law in the settlement agreement. (45)

In addition to the monetary portions of the Settlement Agreement that the Commission rightfully seeks annual reports on, the Developer has several contractual duties to protect the wetlands, to maintain coastal dunes, to construct and maintain a public park, to protect endangered bird species, to limit impacts to the beach and the public by recreational equipment and beach furniture, to promote marine animal awareness to its guests, to ensure proper drainage, to monitor near shore water quality, to limit construct impacts and methods among other items. These obligations are legally to WMPA and WMPA is the only entity that has standing to enforce these obligations.

Unlike some SMA interventions by others, WMPA continues to firmly insist that the terms of the Settlement Agreement be followed and it regularly monitors and investigates the activities of the Developer in relation to its obligations under the settlement agreement in the construction and operation of the resort. Over the years, this has required substantial work by attorneys, engineers, and other experts. This has also included more than one lawsuit over previous conflicts WMPA and the Developer have had regarding the Developer's obligations with respect to building and design. The intent of the funds disbursed to WMPA in 2005 were to pay for these types of on-going enforcement and monitoring expenses and that is exactly what WMPA has been doing and will continue to do until every obligation of the Developer has been satisfied.

In conclusion, the only monies disbursed to WMPA under the Settlement Agreement by the Developer were the monies it was specifically and expressly required to disburse 2005. WMPA will not receive any further disbursements under the Settlement Agreement. The remaining disbursements under the Settlement Agreement have been and will continue to go to third parties.

WMPA hopes that this letter has clarified any confusion that may have been caused by the series of factually erroneous statements made by the aforementioned individuals during the May 28, 2013 Commission meeting.

Very truly yours,
LAW OFFICE OF LANCE D. COLLINS

LANCE D. COLLINS
Attorney for West Maui Preservation Association

c: Michelle C. McLean, Deputy Director
Joseph Prutch, Planner V

3

Index